PASTORAL COUNSELING IN A GLOBAL CHURCH

Voices from the Field

Edited by

ROBERT J. WICKS
BARRY K. ESTADT

ORBIS BOOKS

Maryknoll, New York 10545

The Catholic Foreign Mission Society of America (Maryknoll) recruits and trains people for overseas missionary service. Through Orbis Books, Maryknoll aims to foster the international dialogue that is essential to mission. The books published, however, reflect the opinions of their authors and are not meant to represent the official position of the society.

Library of Congress Cataloging-in-Publication Data

Pastoral counseling in a global church : voices from the field /
  edited by Robert J. Wicks, Barry K. Estadt.
    p. cm.
  Includes bibliographical references.
  ISBN 0-88344-865-3 (pbk.)
  1. Pastoral counseling. 2. Cross-cultural counseling. I. Wicks,
Robert J. II. Estadt, Barry K., 1934- .
BV4012.2.P294 1993
253.5'09—dc20
                                          93-22082
                                            CIP

CONTENTS

INTRODUCTION

Pastoral Counseling in a Global Church is designed to contribute to the dialogue that is now taking place on the important subject of multi-cultural pastoral care. The goal in developing this book was to provide a brief volume in which to gather the *experience* and *impressions* of pastoral counselors involved in ministry in different cultures and countries. In this sense this work is meant to serve as a practical, narrative-style approach to pastoral care and to complement some of the more extensive theoretical treatments of cross-cultural secular and pastoral counseling (Augsburger 1986; Comas-Diaz and Griffith 1988; Sue and Sue 1990).

Each contributor not only has a theological background and extensive ministerial experience but also an advanced degree or teaching experience in pastoral counseling. All have participated in some way in the ecumenical, interdisciplinary graduate programs in pastoral counseling at Loyola College in Maryland. In addition, the contributors are either reflecting upon the country and culture of their origin or upon the country and culture in which they are presently engaged in full-time active ministry. Consequently, in moving from chapter to chapter and section to section, the reader can not only expect the usual variance in style and approach of an edited work but also the richness and diversity arising from the fact that the different countries and cultures are being addressed from differing personal perspectives.

Awareness of the unique challenges, needs, and nuances of people from distinct cultures and countries is especially important in today's pluralistic society. Everything a person says, does, thinks, and experiences must be interpreted through the medium of culture. As a result, sensitivity to how people, their families, and societies are vehicles for their own culture is essential if one is to be helpful to them in any meaningful way.

For persons in ministry this is of increased importance today because, in many areas of the world, mental health professionals are avoided or used only as sources of last resort. Ministers are approached with much more ease and greater frequency. And so, ministers who are able to apply culturally relevant and sensitive pastoral counseling skills are in an ideal position to provide needed holistic psychological-spiritual assistance.

On the other hand, in those cases where sensitivity to the culture values, interpersonal styles, and understanding of the language of those being ministered to is *not* present, the results may be detrimental. At the very least, in such instances the credibility of the pastoral worker will be diminished; in the worst case scenario, such distance or misunderstandings can lead to poor or dangerous consequences. To have a sense of, feel for, or experience of the cultural context of the population being ministered to or treated is essential—whether this ministry of care is being undertaken in the person's country of origin, following immigration, or even after movement by the person to a different part of the country within which he or she now resides.

Too often ministers encounter persons who have moved from one country to another, but because no language shift was required (for example, someone moves from one Spanish-speaking country in Central or South America to another) they may fail to appreciate the upheaval involved, that even though the language is the same, the new culture is still dramatically different. In a similar vein, ministers may not realize how disruptive even a move *within* the same country can be. (Those persons who live in the United States, for instance, and have moved from a rural to an urban setting, or from New York in the north to Selma, Alabama, in the south [or vice versa] would attest to the fact that even moves within one's own land can cause dramatic culturally based stress.) Add those situations in which political and economic factors are different as well—as in the case of moving from Hanoi to the southern part of Vietnam—and one can imagine the stress resulting from even seemingly minor geographic relocations and transitions. Therefore, even the cultural variances within countries must be noted by ministers if the pastoral care undertaken is to be meaningful. Knowing this, we can begin to see the great import, and sense the potentially significant interpersonal rewards, of being attuned to the nuances of cultural diversity.

It is obvious, then, that possibilities to encourage appreciation of the unique talents, customs, styles, and needs of individual peoples throughout the world should be acted upon by those interested in pastoral care. It is with this goal in mind that this simple, illustrative, international "sampler" of the experience of ministers specially educated in pastoral counseling was prepared.

Pastoral Counseling in a Global Church is divided into four broad geographical sections: Central/South America, Africa, the Orient, and Europe/Australia. Following this, a brief epilogue and a special appendix address the experience of two "partners in ministry," who provided a supportive network for persons involved in pastoral care in different parts of the globe.

The reactions to encountering the impressions of the committed ministers in this book will no doubt be as myriad as the persons reading about their experiences. However, as the editors moved through their joys, points of view, suggestions, cautions, "stumblings," ruminations, and ideas, the theme that seemed to pervade the pages—no matter how difficult the circumstances, or varied the settings—was *hope*. It is in this Spirit that we offer you their contributions.

LATIN AMERICA

1

VENEZUELA

JOSEPH HEIM

Father Joseph Heim, M. M., Director of the Social Apostolate for the Diocese of Barinas, Venezuela, coordinates a day clinic, six multi-day care centers, legal services, twenty-one infant survival centers, and spends two afternoons a week in the more formal practice of pastoral counseling.

Aware of the problems inherent in understanding a culture different from one's own, Father Heim calls upon the work of Venezuelan psychologists, anthropologists, and other scholars in his attempt to offer some insights into the dehumanizing impact of the machismo *culture on both men and women.*

Father Heim notes that the all-pervasive faith dimension is passed on through the culture quite independent of the activity of the church. Much of the work of a pastoral counselor, in Venezuela as elsewhere, involves active listening and offering acceptance, understanding, and affirmation. Given the worsening economic outlook, Fr. Heim is convinced that the best way to reach out to the broader population is through the training of lay volunteers.

Pastoral counseling, as such, is virtually unknown in Venezuela. Both the self-concept of the priest and the role into which the laity generally casts him does not include counseling as North Americans would understand the discipline. In 1965 my Spanish teacher, a Venezuelan, explained that in his country the priest is considered rather as a public functionary. He gives a service, and he receives his pay. The increased population and general lack of vocations to the ordained priesthood have aggravated the problem, and the pastor dedicates himself mostly to administrative tasks

3

and the celebration of sacraments. Counseling skills are not among the general expectations that most Venezuelans have of their priests. Moreover, when approached with a personal problem, most clergy tend to give moralistic responses or try to "solve the difficulty." It appears that the future will not be significantly different; no major seminary offers courses in counseling, not even the most advanced and liberal ITER (Theological Institute for Religious Studies) in Caracas.

There is, however, a solid cultural basis for pastoral counseling. Belief in God is part of the very fiber of most Venezuelans. Despite the attempts of agnostic dictators of the nineteenth and twentieth centuries to eradicate religion from the national boundaries, it remains a vital issue. An inscription to the Immaculate Conception still encircles the official seal of the country. What is most important, and difficult, for foreigners to grasp is that, unlike most European and North American experiences, the faith life of the people very often has little or nothing to do with the local parish and the official church. The faith is passed down through local customs. For instance, there is a custom for family and friends to gather for nine nights after a death and burial to pray for the deceased. We have attended many of these "novenarios" and noticed that practically no one present ever entered a local church, yet all knew and answered the prayers in their entirety. Venezuelans, then, are deeply religious persons although their religiosity may not be expressed in formal church practices. Most people have maintained their belief in the supernatural but do not find that the official church practices help them in expressing their beliefs.

Blessings are very important in Venezuela. No child would ever leave his parent's presence or return to it without asking for a blessing. *"Bendición, papá."* The parent (or uncle, aunt, or grandparent) always answers: *"Dios te bendiga, mi hijo."* Just how deeply blessings are a part of the culture came home to us from the experience of a Belgian priest working in one of the largest apartment complexes of Caracas. Father Diego Croen had organized a first communion class, and he visited their homes. In one home he met the father of the child and was informed that they were atheists and that no son of his would be taking part in religion classes. Diego said he understood. The man went on to explain the reasons for his atheism, and Diego continued to listen politely. Finally, the man's son got tired of the conversation and said he was going out to play ball. As he left the house he said, *"Benedición, papá."* And, with no apparent awareness of any contradiction, the father answered, *"Dios te bendiga, mi hijo."* Sra. Angustias lived in a small hut about eleven miles from the closest town in the state of Trujillo where I was visiting friends. When she heard there was a priest in the area she sent for me because she wanted to go to confession. She spoke rather matter-of-factly about her approaching death and showed me her swollen ankles and neck; she knew that she had only a little time to live. What most impressed me, however, was that she was more concerned about dying without a priest than she was about dying. Later that evening, accompanied by about thirty friends and family members, I brought her communion. Traditionally I would have concluded the service with a blessing, but I began to think how much of a blessing she had been for me and for many others. I asked her to give the blessing. Without a moment's hesitation she arose from the chair where she had been propped up by pillows, extended her arms like the pope giving the *urbi et orbi*, made a few remarks about how they should live as Christian neighbors, and then, very grandly, blessed us all. The pastoral counselor, trained abroad, brings important skills to the work in Venezuela, but most of us will be neophytes and learners in deep matters of faith.

To the chagrin of the official church, but in great part due to the lack of clergy, there is a wide-spread belief in spiritism. When the average person experiences a serious personal or interpersonal problem, the first place he or she goes is to a spiritist. This phenomenon probably stems from the need for some relationship to the transcendental in a context where the official church is not always available. Many years ago, while I was working in a housing project in Valencia, a local doctor remarked about the number of spiritists in a neighboring slum. He said, "What would most surprise you is the number of people who drive up there in their LTD or Mercedes Benz—generals, lawyers, even university professors." "Why is that?" I asked. He answered: "Because the spiritist will take time with the person, while priests and doctors are too busy to spend time talking. We lack the human dimension of warmth."

Spiritism has a wide range of meanings, which can include anything from black magic, invoking some evil upon another person, to natural medicines, and even faith healing. The foreigner must be careful not to judge too quickly what is acceptable and what is not in this area. One Sunday after mass in our parish in Caracas, a man asked me to drive him and his two-year-old son to a "woman who cures" about five kilometers outside of the city. He explained that he had taken the boy to the hospital twice in two days. The staff had done absolutely nothing, although the child had been constipated for over three days. Feeling that if I had a son who had received such non-treatment in a hospital, I would probably take him to a spiritist or to anyone who could heal him, I went with them, although I had a lot of anxiety about what sort of situation I was becoming involved in. We found the woman's house, and the father explained his son's problem. She talked for a while, and massaged the baby's stomach for a few minutes before going for some olive oil and then continuing to massage. In the meantime other family members came in and discussed the case. The woman's daughter made some tea from orange leaves and gave it to the baby to drink. The older woman continued to rub the child's stomach. From time to time he would break wind, and then everyone would smile triumphantly. The cure was working. At one point the woman said some quiet prayers and made the sign of the cross three times over the baby's stomach, nothing more arcane than what I or any other priest would have done. It all took about an hour and a half, during which time the woman talked about family and other matters. I remembered what the doctor in Valencia had said, that the spiritist will take time to talk with people and establish a human relationship. As we left, with more orange leaves to make tea at home, the man slipped her a ten bolivar note (about $2.20). It was his offering to her; she had named no price.

However we may consider it, spiritism is a part of the Venezuelan culture, and we must learn to maintain a non-judgmental attitude toward it. The learned Jesuit Juan Ganuza, an expert in ecumenism and in spiritism in Venezuela, told me many years ago that he knows of any number of priests and at least one bishop who consult spiritists.

One further aspect of popular faith in Venezuela is the deep devotion to the Blessed Mother, who at times seems equal to if not superior to the Lord. It is not uncommon for someone to say, "If God wills," only to have another correct him with a stern, "If God *and the Virgin wills*!" Some Northerners are scandalized at this seemingly excessive devotion to the Blessed Mother. Perhaps it is not so excessive; perhaps it is the faith of the people correcting the official faith of a predominately male church. What God has revealed to the little ones and hidden from the wise and learned (Matthew 11:25) is the feminine side of God, that is, the tender and merciful side that the people of simple faith insist upon by their devotion to the mother of God.

These anecdotes and stories, hopefully, provide some feeling for the cultural context in which pastoral counseling must function in Venezuela.

The first of the assumptions that the pastoral counselor can make is that there is an all-pervasive faith dimension to the lives of most Venezuelans. The God Is Dead movement never established any roots in Venezuela but rather was always regarded as some kind of North American or European craziness. Like Job, Venezuelans may get angry at God, argue and complain to God, but outright atheism is relatively uncommon. The processes of urbanization and of technological progress in Venezuela have not produced the crisis of faith that recent decades have witnessed in the more industrialized countries of the First World. The Venezuelan is basically a religious person.

There is a general love for the scriptures and a knowledge of the principal biblical events even among people with no formal religious education. This is a valuable aid for the counselor. It is also entirely acceptable to pray, especially with the sick. Often, while praying with the sick or dying, I have found that they repeat your words, making it their own prayer. In the early years, while still fumbling with the language, I would notice that the sick person would repeat the words of the prayer including my grammatical errors, a testimony to the adaptability of the Venezuelan.

Pastoral Counselors in Venezuela must deal with the expectation that they will "fix up" the problem and, usually, *someone else's* problem. In the early months of our counseling program in Barinas I noticed that many people never showed up for the first appointment. Consulting with the secretary I realized that most people were signing up *other* family members. We had to make a rule that no one could sign up another, and even with that rule we have had a rash of parents who come in hoping to have a child "straightened out." A good number of people, then, look to psychology as a means of changing others.

Seeking help is generally considered a sign of weakness, so few men seek counseling. Most commonly it is the woman, the mother of the family, who is looking for help with one of her children or her husband. In this way she fulfills her role of "family protector."

Also, people look for quick and almost magical answers. It takes a while to help establish confidence in themselves as their own problem-solvers. In part, I believe that this derives from the early formation-education of children. Although Venezuelan parents are very permissive with their little children, allowing them great leeway in their behavior, I have found that most resort to shaming methods as the child nears school age, thus creating self-doubts that make adolescents and adults question their own feelings, ideas, and even their self-worth. The work of John Bradshaw, for example, *Healing the Shame That Binds You*, has been very helpful to me in counseling in Venezuela, especially with the addictive personality (Bradshaw 1988).

It is important to understand how the vast majority of people see the priest and/or pastoral counselor. Since he is usually better educated than the majority of his parishioners, in the poorer areas, at least, he is considered an expert in most matters and especially matters of the psyche (soul, life). Because he is God's representative and holds the title of father, he is considered to have the right answer. There is no need, therefore, for him to ask "What do *you* think?" or "What would *you* like to do?" Most people want a direct answer or solution, and the priest quite readily responds to that expectation.

Another assumption that the pastoral counselor in Venezuela can make is that the process will be short term. Many people only come once or twice. If they return, it will be many months later when another problem has surfaced. Obviously this led to no small amount of self-doubting on my part until I had the courage to mention it to my supervisor, who assured me that it is quite common in the profession, especially among the very poor. One reason is simply economical; they may not have the money for the bus fare to come every week. Also, if they go away feeling good from the first session, they see no reason to return ... until another problem surfaces. Also, as we mentioned in the previous paragraph, the counselor is presumed to be an expert and to have the answers, so most clients do not think in terms of process. They would much prefer a professional "solution" rather than to enter into a process of having to understand their feelings, their hidden agenda, and their relationships.

Any discussion of the *context* of counseling in Latin America must necessarily deal with the question of *machismo*. Some experts, for instance,

Dr. Samuel Roll of the University of New Mexico, claim that *machismo* was originally and should be considered a positive concept. The word *macho* means "male." For Roll, a *macho* is a true man; that is, one who provides for his children, protects women, and would never abuse a member of the weaker sex. A *macho* would give his life in protection of another (Roll 1991). Roll's definition might reflect the reality of an earlier historical period but *machismo* today is generally a negative term; it refers to the man who considers himself the sole boss, the dominator of women, the judge whose word is never challenged, free to do as he pleases, answerable to no one. Actually, *machismo* covers over a deep insecurity, as is evident from one of the most common statements that men make: "I did that so that they would know that I am *macho*." Obviously, the need to prove oneself to another stems from a profound insecurity.

Fr. Ignacio Castillo, a Venezuelan Jesuit and anthropologist, locates the origins of *machismo* in the conquistador. His thesis is that, unlike the pioneers to North America, who emigrated for religious or political reasons and took their wives and families with them to the new land, the Spanish conquistadors, who had just driven the Moors from their homeland and were looking for more lucrative situations, sailed for the new continent leaving their wives behind them. Although they facilitated the implantation of the Catholic faith by the sword, they were not motivated by religious motives; nor did they live celibate lives. They took Indian women as concubines but, of course, could not marry them because they were already legally married in Spain. Therefore, they felt no obligation to the Indian woman and could easily leave her and go on to other conquests, human and material. The situation was basically unstable and continues today in the proliferation of fatherless households.

Left alone with the care of the children, the woman tended to console herself by pouring all of her affection on them, especially the male ones. She spoiled them by treating them as little kings but, at the same time, exercised total domination of them. As the boy grew to manhood, he had to do so without the presence of a male figure and also had to deal with two conflicting (unconscious) feelings: on the one hand, he felt a powerful devotion to his mother, who had done so much for him; on the other hand, he felt a deep resentment toward her because he knows he has been *dominated by a woman*! This latter awareness causes serious doubts about his identity; as an adult, therefore, he has to prove his manhood, and he does so by dominating other women. The excessive devotion to the mother is, in many ways, a reaction to defend himself against his anger at her for dominating him. Since he cannot express his anger at his mother, he demonstrates it by dominating other females.

Machismo influences personal identity and marital relationships. For the most part, a woman's identity is first that of mother and only secondly of woman. This lesson is learned from early childhood: the female's very existence is determined by her capacity for giving birth. The reason so many unmarried girls and women have children is that they cannot countenance life without them. Their very being is intricately tied up with their offspring. There is an economic dimension to this phenomenon in that children are also one's social security, the assurance that old age will not bring loneliness or destitution; but, basically, it is a question of identity. One of the first questions asked of our single lay missionaries is, "Where are your children?" In fact, one young couple who were childless received any number of offers of a child. They were astounded when a woman would say, "Here, take one of mine." (It was always the youngest one that was offered for adoption.)

If the woman's identity is first that of mother, the male's identity is first that of son. Being his mother's son determines his maleness. His relationship with her continues into adult life as the fundamental and all-determining basis for his being. When questioned about his family, the married man will usually mention his mother before his wife and children. From childhood he has had to meet his mother's emotional needs, thereby creating an incestuous relationship in every sense except the genital. The results of this relationship cause serious unconscious conflicts and fears about homosexuality. In fact, most psychologists feel that *machismo* is basically a defense against homosexual feelings resulting from the over-identification of the male with his mother.

The *"machista"* family also affects the adult daughter in that she continues to be closely bonded with the mother but carries out the same dynamics with her children. The power of the mother was brought home to me very vividly many years ago when I attended the baptism of a boy who was named Ricardo Jose after Fr. Dick Albertine and myself. I jokingly said that I was not going to attend the baptism because they had put my name second and Dick's name first. With that, one of the women spoke up and said, "When my daughter has a son I am going to call him Jose Ricardo." What struck me was the freedom that the future grandmother had to name her grandson. No one questioned her right to make that statement; her authority within the family was undisputed.

Dr. Roberto Zapata, a Spanish-born Venezuelan psychologist who has worked for over twenty years in Caracas, holds that, for the most part, there are "not couples but coupling." (Many of the concepts on *machismo* presented here are taken from an unpublished paper by Dr. Zapata.) By that he means that many marriages, legal as well as common law, are unions of convenience that permit the individuals to fulfill their basic needs, but have little view to mutuality. The woman fulfills the one need that the man's mother cannot, that is, his sexual need; the male provides the children and the house that make it possible for the woman to realize a sense of her own identity. The husband does not expect his wife to meet his other emotional needs, since these are met by his mother. The woman, however, is expected to be faithful to the relationship; the man is generally free to follow other "conquests."

The consequences of this system are devastating for human relations in general and for marriages in particular. The man is boss; he does not have to relate to anyone else except on his own terms. As a result, he is often isolated emotionally from his family. To ease the pain of this isolation he seeks company elsewhere, while the woman, in turn, learns to manipulate rather than deal directly in order to have her needs and the needs of her children met. Many home situations fit Thoreau's description of "lives of quiet desperation."

Many young women in our pre-matrimonial courses complained about their early years when "all the rules were for the girls but no restrictions for the boys." They felt the injustice of the system and, indeed, were often victims of what I consider to be the great unnamed secret of Venezuela: incest. Incest is much more prevalent than is generally considered, but the shame involved is so deep that few women will mention the subject.

I will never forget the day nearly twenty years ago when an eighteen-year-old girl ran away from her home in our parish. She left a fifteen-page letter to her mother in which she explained how her father had systematically violated her for over five years. I can still hear the mother's cries. "Is this life?" she asked over and over. After leaving home the girl took up with her employer, who maintained an apartment for her in another city. A few years later she came to visit me and brought her two children with her: a four-year-old boy and a two-year-old daughter. And there, the drama played itself out before my eyes. The little boy spent almost the entire time of the visit hitting or kicking or taking things from his sister. The most that the mother would do was mildly reprimand him and try to protect the girl, but she never put any real limits to his behavior. She was promoting the very system that had practically destroyed her own life.

This is a bleak picture, and it is not inaccurate. We know it is not only a Latin American phenomenon. The feminist movement in the United States has helped many women to voice what they never thought they would be able to explain. John Bradshaw estimates that there are sixty million victims of incest in the United States (Bradshaw 1988).

As I mentioned above, although Venezuelan parents are very permissive with young children, they tend to use excessive shaming techniques when the child nears school age, and many primary school teachers continue the practice in the classroom. One young woman complained about her mother's use of physical punishment and said, "I can understand her insulting me, I know she has to do that, but why does she hit me?" My question, of course, was "Why does she have to *insult* you?" This type of education and formation has disastrous effects on the self-image of the child.

Another element that affects pastoral counseling in Venezuela is the seriously deteriorating economic situation at this time. With a 40 percent inflation rate, the middle and even upper-middle classes are feeling the pinch. The cost of medicine has skyrocketed so much that the average remedy for parasites may consume two or three days salary for an average worker. Many people seem literally stunned by the overpowering economic situation and have become like zombies. About a fourth of the people coming into our center for counseling are really looking for a hand-out. The pastoral counselor in these circumstances becomes more of a pastor or social worker than counselor as he or she attempts to address the wider problem (see below for my ideas about the future of pastoral counseling).

With that background, we will now consider the role of the pastoral counselor in Venezuela. The first thing the pastoral counselor becomes aware of is that he or she is God's representative and that this is God's work. Most people are expecting to be judged, accused, and probably even condemned. So, one of the immediate rewards of this work is to see the relief (after the unbelief!) on the client's face when no criticism, much less condemnation, is forthcoming.

Listening, of course, is essential to the process as the therapist tries to pick up the feeling (or the lack of feeling), and the patterns, and then gently offers them for consideration. Most people have already talked the presenting problem over with a friend or acquaintance and have gotten advice on what they should feel and do. They expect the counselor to do the same and are invariably surprised when the counselor responds by asking them about their options. As the process continues, the client becomes more and more aware of his or her own feelings in an accepting atmosphere, feelings that the person never knew existed. To be a part of that process is one of the most rewarding experiences in counseling.

Perhaps it is the frustrated professor in me, but I often find it necessary to explain two truths to clients. The first truth is that feelings are not bad; if anything, they are good because they are human. Many people confuse the feeling with the action; they *feel* guilty when they have not *done* anything. For instance, most people seem convinced that anger is a sin. It is often necessary to explain that the feeling is not bad or good, it is what we do with the feeling that is bad or good. Thank heaven that the evangelists had the good sense to include Jesus' cleansing of the Temple. I have probably used that more than any other biblical event in counseling.

The other truth I often explain is that feelings follow thoughts. The only way to change a feeling is to examine and change the thought that produced the feeling. I am indebted to Rollo May's *Love and Will* (1969) and Ellis and Harper's *A New Guide to Rational Living* (1975) for these insights. They have been very helpful in guiding clients to examine the rationality of the thought. Then the feeling usually takes care of itself in an anxiety-free manner. This approach overcomes the antiquated and terribly frustrating attempts to use will power as a way of changing a feeling.

One of the most enlightening clarifications I have read on the role of the trans-cultural counselor is David Augsburger's concept of interpathy (Augsburger 1986). Beyond sympathy—the ability to feel what another feels—and beyond empathy—the ability to communicate to another that you feel what he or she feels—lies the task of the cross-cultural therapist;

that is, to place oneself in the world view and the value system of the other without necessarily abandoning one's own value system or world view.

> In interpathic caring, I, the culturally different, seek to learn and fully entertain within my consciousness a foreign belief. I take a foreign perspective, base my thought on a foreign assumption, and allow myself to feel the resultant feelings and their cognitive and emotive consequences in my personality as I inhabit, insofar as I am capable of inhabiting, a foreign context. Interpathy is the voluntary experiencing of a separate other without the reassuring epistemological floor of common cultural assumptions; it is the intellectual invasion and emotional embracing of what is truly other (Augsburger 1986, 30).

One example of interpathy for me is belief in ghosts. I do not personally believe in them, but most Venezuelans do. However, I can assume that stance and relate to that reality without too much trouble. A lay missionary who worked in our Caracas barrio parish, Marianne Smith of Stockton, California, was a natural at interpathy, although she had never heard the word. She had a gift for identifying with others in their world view while also being able to speak gently of options. When it came to raising women's consciousness about their dignity and rights, she realized that some actually got beaten when they tried to assert themselves at home. What was she to do? She realized that it was not she who was suffering the consequences. How do you evangelize from an interpathic position when to evangelize means to bring good news, and that news is by its very nature something new, not part of the accepted culture? The notion of interpathy reminds us of the great caution and respect that is necessary in any counseling situation, but especially counseling in a trans-cultural context.

Counseling in Venezuela has occasioned some new experiences. For instance, confidentiality is not so important an issue as it is in the United States. One reason is simply that the poor do not have the luxury of much privacy, and nearly everyone knows everyone else's problems. While walking through our barrio in Barinas one day, a woman standing in front of her house asked to speak to me. As we sat down I noticed her two daughters, nine and ten years old, sitting on the floor playing. She began to talk about her problem of not being able to get on a bus or into a car for fear that she would die; as she continued to explain the symptoms, her daughters chimed in with other symptoms, for example, of how she was terrified of a rain storm and would hide under the bed when it thundered. Although she tried to pretend that the children were exaggerating, she did not deny what they said or seem to mind their being present. With the children still present she began to talk about her one-year-old son. She explained that she had not wanted to become pregnant and that one month after his birth, he nearly died from a stomach disorder. It was obvious that the near death of the child had triggered unconscious guilt feelings, and her anxiety attacks were due to her fear of being punished. We talked it out and prayed. The little girls were present the entire time. I was conscious of their presence and a bit uncomfortable because of the delicacy of the matter discussed, but since the woman seemed comfortable I saw no reason to try to change the location or to ask the girls to leave.

As mentioned before, men come to counseling only when they are hurting very badly. A few years ago a man came in with his wife; he was so depressed that he could not drive a car. By the third session he began to feel a little better, but then he wanted to change the nature of our relationship. He wanted to be friends. He thought we should continue to talk, but at his house, where we could have a few beers, and so on. Now, Venezuelans are very personable people and relationships are important to them. I thought of complying, thinking that it would be a more "Venezuelan" way of doing therapy, but then I reconsidered because I knew I would not be comfortable in that situation. He did not come back for any more sessions.

Women often try to second-guess and thus simply don't hear what is being said. The most direct and simple statement will be interpreted in an entirely different way than intended. I think the origin of this symptom is that women have had to "get around" men in order to survive in a *macho* society. Women's lives are often not their own. Any male member of the family, even a younger brother, can order them around or send them on errands. One young woman, a twenty-two-year-old university student, wanted to break off with her fiancé but could not because her father was indebted to the young man for a favor done. The father actually forbade her to break the engagement. The young man would come by each day, and she would have to make him a meal, wash his clothes, and, on occasion, even miss class if he wanted her to run an errand. Only when she began to face her options and realize that she could handle her father's threat of expulsion from the home did she finally decide to stand up for her rights and break off the relationship. The father was not happy, but he did not throw her out.

I believe that the majority of clients experience a sense of relief from counseling. They expect to be judged and are surprised when they are not. Many make heavy projections onto their therapists, feeling that we know them "inside and out," even though we often experience doubts and uncertainties. Those who come with children who are acting-out are usually disappointed when the counselor does not join in blaming the child; some do not return, especially when we suggest a look at the whole family picture. In general, however, I have been impressed with the confidence that most people show toward the counselor. The majority seem to open up very quickly, perhaps due to the degree of pain that has brought them to therapy.

I do not think that the process of pastoral counseling in Venezuela differs to any significant degree from that in other countries. We try to follow the fundamental principles of active listening, naming the patterns and offering them for consideration, and helping to consider options. Much of the work of a therapist is the same as that of a missionary, namely, the affirmation of the uniqueness of the person. What is specific to pastoral counseling is the incorporation of the faith life of both client and therapist in the process. The scriptures, stories of the heroes of faith, imposition of hands, prayers, and blessings are all valuable assets in the process of pastoral counseling.

I must admit to a certain distrust of religious language, perhaps because of the tendency of so many people (including myself) to hide behind religious or psychological terminology. The difficult part is to ascertain, without being judgmental, just how well the religious theme has been integrated into the client's life or how much it is a shield against life. The best indicator seems to be the level of anxiety that accompanies the statement. Tension and anxiety generally point to a non-integration of the theme because Jesus' message was so often: "Do not be anxious," "Do not be afraid," "Peace be with you," "Why are you afraid?" However, just how to challenge in this area is still a matter of personal search.

Silences have always been able to hook my own insecurities, but I have found that to the extent that I become comfortable with them, the client becomes more reflective, senses a greater freedom, and almost always looks more deeply within. Because they are used to waiting and do not share our North American need to produce results, most Venezuelans are not upset by silences; with them I have learned how rich the non-verbal can be.

To elaborate a theory of pastoral counseling for Venezuela would require a longer presentation than the present context permits. However, in conjunction with the general Rogerian approach, in which I personally believe, I would also suggest several insights from a few of the more recent developments in the field of counseling.

First, the family systems approach developed by Minuchin, Haley, and others has proven very helpful to our work here in Venezuela, in part because it reflects the thinking of the theologians of liberation. One must consider not only the individual but the context in which the individual lives and operates; change is brought about not only by dealing with the person but by trying to affect the structure that affects the person. The systems approach is a quick way of doing therapy, with no apology for that adjective. Our present situation is a small center for social services in the diocese of Barinas, a rural state with approximately 360,000 inhabitants. There are nine consulting psychologists, all at master's level, and three psychiatrists in the entire state. We do not have the luxury of long-term therapy. The insights of the systems method have been immensely helpful. For instance, an eighteen year old came in for help because her four-year-old son was acting-out. She was separated from her husband and living with her parents; two older brothers resided in the same house. To the question, "How many people have authority over this child?" she responded that, since they were all adults, everyone in the house exercised some kind of authority over the child. I responded: "So he has no father and ... " as I continued to say " ... he has too many fathers," she understood and actually said the words with me. We then talked about the ways in which she could elicit the support of her family but maintain the sole responsibility for her child's formation.

The works of John Bradshaw quoted above and his taped television series have provided important insights into counseling in the Venezuelan context, because he has laid open the matter of shame in society. As I have mentioned elsewhere, my impression is that in Venezuela most parents are very permissive with the child in the early years (thus establishing some base for identity later in life), but as the child reaches school age the method shifts to shaming. Much of primary education continues with the shaming methodology—solving immediate problems for the teacher but with permanent damage to the child. The stories of so many addictive personalities reflect deep shame. The inability of some men to show affection to their wives stems from the deep conviction that they are not worth loving; they fear that any demonstration of affection on their part will be rejected. Some recent works on crisis intervention, especially by Aguilera and Messick and by Eugene Kennedy, have provided valuable tools for counseling in the Venezuelan situation. Kennedy is more pastoral and uses many practical examples, while Aguilera and Messick provide excellent visual methods for an approach to crises. We have used these very effectively in teaching groups of lay persons how to intervene and *how not to intervene* in times of tragedy.

One other discipline that has proved helpful to our work is neurolinguistic programming. My basic texts are *The Structure of Magic* (Bandler and Grinder 1975) and *Frogs Into Princes* (Bandler and Grinder 1979). These works have helped me not to presume that I understand the meaning of the words the client uses but always to attempt to get more clarity. As clients are gently pushed to examine their own thoughts they seem, almost automatically, to get into their own feelings. One middle-aged couple came in for help because they were having a lot of difficulties since the wife's surgery for a brain tumor. She felt that they were drifting apart and that her husband was insensitive. As he explained *his side* of the problem he described the night, a year previously, when he had come home from work and found her collapsed on the floor. As he said the words "lying there on the floor," he seemed to be sneering. I was shocked, of course, at his reaction and asked if we could back up for a moment and go over that part again. He repeated the sentence with the same emphasis, so I asked "What were you feeling when you found your wife lying there on the floor?" He hesitated for a second and then, to the surprise of both his wife and myself, he began to weep uncontrollably. Then he began to share, for the first time, the terror he had felt that she might die.

Concerning the future of pastoral counseling in Venezuela I must limit my remarks to my present situation, that is, director of pastoral services in a rural diocese where I dedicate two afternoons a week to counseling. Due to the lack of trained professionals in the mental health field in the state of Barinas and considering the ever-worsening economic situation, we must look beyond counseling on an individual basis and consider ways to reach the wider population through the mass media and by training lay persons. For instance, our state has the nation's second highest rate of suicide among women, so we must look for ways to do preventive work through the press and the radio.

One goal should be to train the clergy to do counseling, but the great majority are obligated, for financial reasons, to dedicate themselves to chaplaincy and/or teaching positions in addition to parochial duties. The majority simply do not see the need for any training beyond what they received in the seminary.

We have tried to offer workshops to apostolic groups, such as the Legion of Mary, Cursillistas, and the catechumenate movement, but with no success to date. However, we have been able to organize courses for groups of catechists, base Christian communities, the local cooperative movement, a women's group, and the caring mothers in a government day care center. These courses have been mostly concerned with human relations, psychosocial development of children, crisis intervention, psychological consequences of the situation of oppression, and transactional analysis.

The future is going to consist in helping non-professionals to develop their natural talents in caring for one another. The delicate part will be not to contaminate them with jargon but enable them to understand what they do when they reach out to others, and to affirm them in their natural abilities. They quite naturally bring the faith dimension into their relationships and could probably give the rest of us lessons in that area. As for the local mental health professionals, I believe that they are people of faith and probably do pastoral counseling quite unawares.

2

PANAMA

GERALDINE BRAKE

Sister Geraldine Brake, M.M., after a decade of missionary work in the war-torn country of Nicaragua between 1972 and 1982, went to Panama, where she hoped to find a more peaceful setting in which to minister. Instead, she found herself in the midst of the American invasion of Panama in December 1989.

In this chapter, Sister Gerri provides an account of her daily work with a group of eighty homeless elderly people who sought safety in a high school building during the peak hours of the American invasion.

As Coordinator of Ocean Breeze, a residence for the most needy senior citizens in Panama, Sister Geraldine continues to dedicate herself to help provide a place where senior citizens can share their lives in an atmosphere of respect and dignity.

I begin this chapter on a small excursion boat headed for the small island of Tobaga, an hour boat ride from Panama City. The scenic route on the Pacific Ocean travels under the Bridge of the Americas, a land bridge between North and South America. It is not only a bridge of land, but of flora, fauna, and humankind. Bridging means that people come and go. And that has been Panama's sociological destiny from the time it was first claimed by the Spanish. *Panama*, in the language of the indigenous, meant "abundance of fish."

The scenic trip and quiet time in Topaga enabled me to pause for a day to look back at the city where I have lived for almost three years. Like Jesus, I value the time apart to reflect on the meaning of life. Much has occurred in this country of 2,418,000 men and women of various ethnic and indigenous backgrounds.

My life has been graced because I have come to know and love many Panamanian people. As I reflect on this three-year experience of Panama, the backdrop of my previous mission in Nicaragua is very present. My first assignment was to Nicaragua from 1972 through 1982. These were crucial years for Nicaraguans as they survived an earthquake, a drought, and an insurrection. There was so much to learn and to challenge the human spirit. I was privileged to be a part of a country that came to claim itself.

A multiplicity of experiences preceded my formal studies at Loyola College in 1982. My final thesis was an integration of my learnings in Nicaragua and the clinical experiences at a local state university in Baltimore. Whether it is focusing on the plight of Nicaraguan people for freedom or the challenges facing young university students in the United States, the search for meaning in life is a universal desire. In the words of the philosopher Nietzche, a person "who has a why to live can bear with almost any how."

Now, several years later, I am reflecting on the same search for meaning but in the culture of Panama. The previous experiences paved the road to Panama for me. The countries are different, and yet so similar. The reflections that follow center on my experiences of working daily with a group of eighty elderly people, left homeless the night of December 19, 1989, during the invasion of Panama by the United States. This group was a small segment of the ten thousand people affected that night in the section of Chorrillo. They all had escaped burning flames and heavy fighting to migrate to a high school building nearby in Balboa. My ministry of pastoral counseling begins at this moment and with these people whom I have been helping to rebuild their lives.

CULTURAL AND THEOLOGICAL FOUNDATIONS
OF PASTORAL COUNSELING

My personal theology of pastoral counseling is reflective of the prophetic concern for acting justly, loving mercifully, and walking humbly with God. Persons seek pastoral counseling when they are in emotional and spiritual pain. Inwardly, they are frightened, guilty, angry, and hurting. These experiences are symptoms indicating that the inner quality of their lives does not bring satisfaction and fulfillment. Instead of inner peace, they experience conflict; instead of joy, they know sadness; instead of love, they feel anger; and instead of possessing a clear vision, they are baffled and perplexed. My concern as a pastoral counselor is with the quality of life, the inner condition. The counselor's primary task is to deal with the person's actual condition as he or she experiences it. I tread softly before those I care for in pastoral counseling. I never want to rush in and solve a problem. I desire to treat others as I would want to be treated. The counselee almost seems to be saying: Look at my life's situation and reflect with me as I search for alternatives. Be with me and for me.

The gospel example of Jesus meeting the Samaritan woman at the well is an inspiring example for me. The woman came to fill her earthen jar with water and encountered Jesus, with his unassuming manner. She obviously sensed understanding in his eyes and felt at ease with him. She came to trust a complete stranger. His tenderness melted her pride, and she shared her cares and concerns. The intimacy between them was sacred. She was honest with him and did not feel ashamed of her past. Jesus was not shocked with anything that she told him. He listened attentively and said he knew all about her life. He called her forth from shame to self-esteem. His honesty freed her as a person. Healing took place.

The woman at the well was transformed once Jesus revealed himself to her. He understood her pain, and he knew that she had sinned. He loved her despite any of her weaknesses. Jesus, the wounded healer, touched the woman deeply, healing her through compassion, understanding, and gentleness. This attitude of Jesus toward others is my hope for myself as a pastoral counselor.

The account of the woman at the well is the basis for my theology of helping in pastoral counseling. I first recognize my own need to be filled by the waters of life, and I strive to accompany others here in Panama to the well for refreshment and a new zest for life.

My pastoral experiences both in Nicaragua and presently in Panama are teaching me volumes about journeying with and helping others. In the face of persecution and hardships of all kinds, the only solid thing to rely on at times is the moral and spiritual support of others. I find that when people are able to express their fears and limitations it is easier to identify with them and to support them in their weakness and fear. The more that I express my fears, the more I deepen my bonds with others.

Strength and healing often come when we are vulnerable. The woman at the well was extremely vulnerable and feeling alone until she discovered the healing presence of Jesus. I endeavor through my life as a pastoral counselor to provide an atmosphere that says whatever the past of the other has been, it is acceptable to be human, to recognize one's gifts as well as one's limitations.

My mind drifts back to the memories of the first days after the invasion. Each morning brought the new dawn, but also the rude awakening of a painful reality of tremendous loss. The homeless people of Chorrillo were tired, hungry, and thirsty. The surroundings of the refuge center was the well where they came to drink of life and satisfy the insatiable thirst for health and security.

THE CONTEXT OF COUNSELING

The context of my counseling experiences has been the setting up and administering of the temporary housing of the elderly people of Chorrillo.

After the initial week of occupying a local high school building and its adjoining stadium, collaborative efforts were made between the authorities of the United States and Panama to locate the more than five thousand homeless in a temporary site while efforts were made to construct houses for them. The site chosen was the Albrook Air Field, and two large hangars were conditioned for shelter for one thousand families. The needs of the elderly were considered. They were housed in an adjacent building; half of the building was used for a clinic and the other half for their residence. The latter consisted of one large room and a bathroom with four toilets and four showers. Right from the first moment we organized the setting to be as comfortable and cheery as possible. Army double beds were cut in half, and everyone had his or her own bed. A mental attitude of privacy was necessary, because life was in the open. How would they sustain themselves for a year waiting for a solution to their housing? I could read fear and distress on the people's faces. They had lost all their earthly possessions; for some this included their eye glasses and dentures. Their shared experience of loss became their greatest bond. I will never forget the spirit of collaboration among the elderly as they made so many adjustments in their lives. Change is never easy; it is even more difficult for the elderly. They were miles away from their hometown of Chorrillo, in the vicinity of the military headquarters. The area in general had mostly wooden condemned buildings where people lived without light or water. Our people were accustomed to living in very poor conditions. Fires were always a threat, as was the case on the night of the invasion.

The population of our elderly community was heterogeneous. There was a cross section of well and sickly men and women. Some had serious illnesses and physical limitations. For instance, there were eight blind people and two borderline tuberculosis patients. A small group suffered from venereal diseases. There were at least four who had serious psychotic disorders. The age range was from fifty to one hundred years of age; two celebrated their one-hundredth birthday during the year of our time together. Their cultural backgrounds varied from various Caribbean islands—Haiti, Jamaica, Barbados, and Grenada. The one unifying factor was their history of poverty. After the initial weeks of eating army rations, an attempt was made to vary the menus according to the various accustomed foods among the group.

ASSUMPTIONS OF PASTORAL COUNSELING

It was evident to me that the crisis situation was calling forth the best in all of us who surfaced to accompany and help these dear people of God. If people were to live together in such close confines, a spirit of harmony was essential. From the first day of settlement, personal responsibility was encouraged, and community-building began. Consultations and communal-decision making became a way of life. The group established a weekly assembly time, every Wednesday afternoon after the lottery. This was the moment to air complaints, make suggestions for improvement, and reflect together on some encouraging theme. Topics discussed ranged from accepting feelings to the need for drinking water.

One volunteer decorated a bulletin board with the words *God Is Love*. What she did spontaneously became the focus of our community experience. There is a God, who is unconditional in fatherly compassion and motherly tenderness. The words helped to focus our reality. The daily expressions of this love never ceased in the providence of so much human kindness and generosity. The community grew in this realization of love, and it made all the difference in the spirit of everyone. As a pastoral counselor with the responsibility of coordinating the over-all operation of the residence, I wondered about my particular gift of service in this crisis situation. It was obvious that what counted was a comforting voice, a smile, a helping hand, and a good listening ear. The presence of innumerable volunteers of different backgrounds injected security and hope into the situation. A core team of eight of us worked on a daily basis with the added support of other volunteers on a shorter basis. We met weekly to reflect on our experiences, to learn from them, to coordinate our efforts, and to encourage one another. We were a tremendous bank of resources, and the motivation to serve others was very deep in the men and women of our team.

Our peer experience allowed us to serve more freely and wisely. We all faced our limitations and strove to balance our energies. The large room was an arena of human needs that could overwhelm a person in the helping ministry. We learned together that all the problems could not be solved, but that we could be present in support and provide for the basic human needs of food and shelter. One team member did a tremendous job of maintaining the place so it was clean and free of offensive odors. The fact that our team was comprised of many young people also made a bright difference. The rapport between young and old served as a unifying dimension.

THE ROLE OF THE PASTORAL COUNSELOR

I found the work naturally appealing, and I desired to dedicate myself full-time to the plight of this group. I took a leave of absence from my regular job in the Office of Ministry in the Archdiocese of Panama to allow me freely to pursue the general coordination of the residence for the eighty senior citizens. My role as a pastoral counselor flowed with the days as I used the best of my creative and professional skills to respond daily to the innumerable challenges.

Coordination of all the services was essential in such a set-up. The entities involved in servicing the needs of our groups were the Ministry of Health of Panama, with a core group of doctors, nurses, and nurses' aides, a full-time social worker, and the representatives of the United States A.I.D. office. From the beginning I scheduled weekly meetings with these service members to facilitate the smooth running of the residence. The medical staff attended to the many health needs. We discussed individuals in relation to the whole picture, always with the desire to work together for the welfare of the person. The presence of the social worker was valuable in reporting the history of the person. Our bonds of confidence and respect deepened, enabling us to minimize any differences of opinions or conflicts of interest that occurred.

An example of united efforts would be Kathleen, a 62-year-old woman who had a long history of psychotic behavior. Most of the time she maintained her sanity through daily doses of tranquilizers. Unlike other active persons in the community, the best we could ask of Kathleen was her cooperation in eating in the dining room and maintaining her personal hygiene. Unfortunately, on three different occasions Kathleen lost her mental balance and became harmful both to herself and others. The decision to hospitalize her was made together, and we coordinated the particulars of her discharge to the hospital. In such an open atmosphere I was concerned always for her sense of dignity when it was necessary to restrain her. I requested an ambulance to come during a meal time when the atmosphere could be private for Kathleen. On all three occasions Kathleen left and returned with a minimum of spectators. She was always returned to the residence, where she obviously felt welcomed and accepted.

Kathleen needed all our concerns, medically and pastorally. The doctors prescribed, but our staff and group lived and interacted with her. An interesting fact about Kathleen is that English is her first language. Very few other than myself spoke English, so I needed to be the prime communicator with her. Gradually there was more and more verbal response from Kathleen.

THE EXPERIENCE OF THE PASTORAL COUNSELOR

Never have I been in a situation that I have loved so much as this experience of accompanying our community of elderly people. In coming to know and love people twice my age, I learned through osmosis the innate wisdom of the age and a certain contemplative attitude toward life. The spirit of joy and an appreciation for the little things of life were contagious and allowed me to experience another aspect of living through these people. Here was a group that had innate patience with waiting: waiting for their housing solution, waiting for family members who often never surfaced, waiting for whatever presented itself during their day. These people had the gift of time: time to enjoy one another's company, time to pray, time to be quiet, time to play cards or dominos, time to quilt a pillow or spread. Their influence keeps adding quality to my life. I am in a humanizing process of growing interiorly.

Initially a group of volunteers organized activities for arts and crafts, offering a variety of crafts according to the interests and individual capabilities. This began a whole way of life for personal enjoyment and satisfaction. My own interests in arts and crafts was ignited. What began for personal enjoyment became a means of public relations and financial support. Through the development of talents we were able to organize a self-help program. We began to display the crafts and sell them for financial support of the residence. Quilting was introduced to the women, and this became the specialty of the house. The women decided on a name for their crafts—Flower of Life. They chose the name to symbolize how they felt about the flowering in their lives. Through this program a sense of pride and dignity has been achieved. The local media has made great propaganda about our talented women.

An important part of this experience has been the contact with all the volunteers who appeared at our open door. I strove to facilitate their presence according to their individual talents and interests. Those who offered to lend a helping hand were encouraged to spend time visiting and seeing the many aspects of the life. Afterward they were invited to serve according to their desire. One volunteer developed a reading group with the blind and others who could not read. She chose great literature, such as *The Good Earth* by Pearl Buck, to read and then have dialogue with the group. Afterward she served a cold juice and cookies. How the group looks forward to her weekly visit! Another volunteer preferred to serve the lunch meal daily and help the people who needed assistance getting to the dining room, which we set up conveniently outside the building with picnic benches.

THE EXPERIENCE OF THE CLIENT

For most of the community the crisis had many redeeming qualities. Many now had a better roof over their head and the constant security of both love and attention. Three good meals a day helped many restore their health. A general sense of well-being increased by the day. Most important was the community experience, the ability to share their plight with others and to create one voice to help resolve their problems. Many increased their faith in God and people through all the manifestations of love. The pastoral efforts of many volunteers, including two dedicated priests, made a great difference. The expressions of faith were very ecumenical; believers from various denominations appeared to add their comfort. Difference in beliefs didn't seem to matter. Most of the population is Catholic, and there were weekly masses. There were always willing volunteers who served by sharing faith with the community. All this added to the spirit of the house.

The living quarters and the constant contact with one another was certainly a new experience for the community. The efforts toward harmony had to be constant to maintain the mental health of the group. Many personalities had very aggressive tendencies. It was my custom to handle all interpersonal conflicts with dialogue. I set aside time for dialogue between both parties. Through the surfacing of their feelings, people tried to listen to the other's point of view. Working through raw feelings and reactions took time and patience. Whenever possible the social worker was present with me, and we both would encourage the persons to solve their own differences. Occasionally it was necessary to have a male presence for protection when there was a tone of violence. Thank God we never resorted to police involvement. A few times certain men chose to leave the premises and fight out their differences.

New friendships were a gift of the time. Victor, a 27-year-old Cuban, presented himself right from the beginning as a volunteer. He became part of the core team, which worked daily at the residence. Victor endeared himself to the people through his gentle spirit and humorous ways. He was an example of responsibility in the over-all operation of the house. After seven full months of collaborating so closely, Victor and his family were given the freedom to move to Miami, Florida. A big party for his departure was prepared, and there were so many expressions of love and appreciation for this valiant person. One resident referred to him as the Angel Raphael from the Book of Tobit; many considered Victor a real angel of God. In dealing with all our feelings of loss in the departure of Victor, I remember with such tenderness the afternoon we shared our tears and feelings for what Victor had been for the community. Victor was still present, so it was also helpful to him. What I liked about the moment was the license that we gave to one another to cry and feel the loss. A safe and sacred atmosphere had been created. The transference between Victor and the group was strong. He had been life and security for them. This experience made all of us involved more human and loving. We captured the moment and felt it deeply.

The experiences of the residents were many and varied. Much energy was derived through the human gathering of love, pain, joy, and challenge.

THE PROCESS OF PASTORAL COUNSELING

I am very aware that my experiences as a pastoral counselor are unique. They are a far cry from my year of clinical experiences on a one-to-one approach. I am not writing about clients in the normal sense of the word. My challenge is to respond in another culture and a particular moment of history. The process leads to the same end of helping others search for alternatives in their lives. This process was described by the late Archbishop Oscar Romero of El Salvador as the theology of accompaniment. He and my own sisters, Maura Clarke and Ita Ford of Maryknoll, along with Dorothy Kazel and Jean Donovan, exemplified a story of love. They were willing to walk the extra mile with others. I derive much strength from knowing and loving them. As psalm 73 says, "They did not forget the life of God's poor ones."

During the last three years in Panama I have thought of the writings of Viktor Frankl, psychiatrist and the originator of the school of existential analysis. Frankl's theory is not an intellectual exercise. It was formed during his experience in Nazi concentration camps during World War II and his living through one of the worst human horrors of modern times. Frankl truly lived his theories. His book *From Death Camp to Existentialism* is a testimony about his experiences to actualize the highest value, to fulfill the deepest meaning, the meaning of suffering. Most of what he believed was essential to life had been stripped away and was found to be unnecessary. For example, Freud's theory of the importance of sexual drive was found to be less than valid, for the prisoners gave little thought to sex, but dreamed of food, warmth, rest, sleep, and loved ones. Frankl's survival was surely a miracle (Frankl 1959).

I identify with Frankl both from experiences during the insurrection of Nicaragua and the one here in Panama. Our community of elderly people had been stripped of all their material goods, and what they desired was food, warmth, rest, sleep, and loved ones. Human life, under any circumstances, does not cease to have a meaning. Life includes suffering, dying, privation, and death. Frankl asked his companions in the camps to face the seriousness of their position. They could not lose hope but had to strive to keep their courage in the certainty that the hopelessness of their struggle did not detract from its dignity and its meaning.

The campsite of the people from Chorrillo was not a concentration camp, but there were similarities in the human quest for meaning. Freedom, after all, is the ability to choose one's attitude in a given set of circumstances. I saw many of our community chose life over death. They survived well because they believed in life and the ultimate mystery of God.

TOWARD A THEORY OF COUNSELING

Having seen life both in Nicaragua and Panama at its best and its worst enables me to understand more deeply other people's struggle with freedom. The central theme of existentialism is that to live is to suffer and to survive is to find meaning in the suffering. If there is a purpose in life at all, there must be a purpose in suffering and dying. Each person must find himself or herself and accept the responsibility that his or her answer prescribes. If the person succeeds, he or she will continue to grow in spite of indignities.

The Existentialists help define my approach to pastoral counseling. Their emphasis on the uniquely human qualities in all people—freedom, choice, valuing, awareness, creativity, and the distinctiveness of each individual— is true to my basic orientation toward life. Therapy aims at helping people develop their authentic being in the world; it seeks to encourage people to learn to confront and cope constructively with their problems.

Additionally, the existential approach relates closest to my personal theology. The emphasis on the potential power of one's future is closely linked with the awareness that hope has tremendous energy for motivating human change. In the last months I have witnessed people facing what looked like a hopeless situation. I saw despair and courage manifested in its highest form. The communal therapy was for each individual to take charge of his or her own life. The spirit of responsibility that existed in our residence paved the road to greater self-satisfaction and pride. This experience made many of us dream of a permanent residence for elderly people based on the style and spirit of our large room.

As the months went by, solutions for housing were resolved. Ten members have died with dignity and grace. With the exception of eight men and women, the others have all left and started anew in a new house. Many have relocated to other areas of Panama, where housing developments have been constructed. After eighteen months together, it is a warm experience to meet one of the community on the street or receive a visit from one of them. Most of them are now living with their families.

The dream of a permanent residence has come of age. Through the miracle of many events and the support of many people who believe in our work, the Ministry of Health has offered us the use of its installations and grounds for the new location of a permanent residence. In January 1991 we transferred from the temporary location to Palo Seco Hospital, located on a beach, facing the entrance to the Panama Canal. The area is a paradise with a magnificent view of the ocean and the transit of ships. The hospital was built by the United States in 1904 to respond to the need of some workers in the Canal who had contracted leprosy. The hospital has served as a healing place for several hundred persons in the last century. With the progress made in the disease, all cases are in remission. Presently the patients are referred to as those with the Hansen's sickness. The United States ran the hospital until 1979, when the Carter-Torrijos treaty was signed. The hospital is now run by the Ministry of Health of Panama. There is only a core group of thirteen elderly patients, who have lived almost their whole lives at this hospital.

In the last months we have been bridging the two groups together— those of the hospital and those of Chorrillo who have no family or place to go. They have all opted to live at the hospital. The first change that was suggested by the patients—who are no longer considered patients—was to change the name. They have felt social rejection by people because of their disease. A contest took place and the name *Brisa del Mar* (Ocean Breeze), was chosen. The residence is a new option for the increasing population of elderly in Panama.

THE FUTURE OF PASTORAL COUNSELING

The future is happening as the days progress. It has been heartwarming to experience the integration of the two groups. We are presently housing twenty-five elderly men and women. The whole setting speaks of peace and tranquility for the garden time of the residents' lives. There are many repairs needed in the buildings. As we make the necessary improvements, we will increase our capacity for residents. We would like to keep the size close to a hundred so as not to lose the family-like atmosphere. We have chosen not to advertise so we can begin slowly but surely. Word has been spreading, and we receive calls and visits from interested senior citizens daily.

The future is bound to be bright. The development of a dream based on a need has been an adventure. The volunteers involved at the Albrook campsite helped form the Foundation of New Life. This foundation is committed to the welfare of the most needy senior citizens in Panama. After many months of organizing, the foundation now has legal status; Brisa del Mar is the first project they will finance. I am a member of the foundation and acting coordinator of Brisa del Mar. As coordinator, I want to keep the vision alive.

As a pastoral counselor, I hope to continue to develop my people skills and deepen my understanding of the culture and the language of the people of Panama. The road has curved and changed in many unexpected ways. With the same trust in God and the goodness of others, I am encouraged to continue in this worthwhile endeavor and ministry. Daily I am fed by the experiences of knowing some of God's choicest persons.

AFRICA

3

KENYA

JOHN RIESCHICK

John Reischick, M.M., Maryknoll brother, writes poignantly of the experi-
ence of leaving his homeland to serve and live amoung the people of Kenya.
John's growth and development into the culture brought a sensitive aware-
ness of profound differences in perception. He shares with the reader his
insights regarding the search of the people of Kenya for an African-Kenyan
identity within the complex convergence of Western values and the Pan-
African movement. John stresses the need for the prospective cross-cultural
counselor to continue in a learning posture and recommends eliciting the
ongoing assistance of a "cultural informant" who can provide a "window"
into the host culture.

On July 13, 1991, nineteen teenage girls were murdered and another
seventy-one raped at a state-run boarding school near Meru, in Kenya. If
the rapes had been all, it's quite possible that no "fuss" would have been
made. Outside of the families, no one would have really cared, and no one
would even have been surprised.

The horrific deaths, however, have sparked off an agonized debate about
the nature of modern Kenyan society. People are searching for an explanation of this seemingly inexplicable tragedy.

To the young, it is more proof of the intolerable pressures that an overloaded curriculum and overcrowded schools put on students. Riots and
disturbances are common now in Kenya. A planned strike at this school,
which led to the slaughter, was the result of some boys being banned the
previous day from attending a sports meeting because of non-payment of
activity fees (the cost of public education is a major problem for poor

families). In fact, this particular district had twenty-one student strikes before the tragedy took place.

To ruling politicians, the tragedy is proof of a breakdown in discipline, a breakdown they conveniently blame on the growing movement to end the country's authoritarian one-party state. Since June 1990 a battle has been raging over political pluralism in Kenya. On one side is a movement dedicated to restoring multi-party democracy and freeing a once vibrant economy now staggering under the weight of corruption. On the other side is President Daniel Arap Moi (KANU), who came to power in 1978 and imposed a constitutional ban on multi-party politics four years later. Only in December of 1991, following intense opposition especially from ex-KANU politicians, lawyers, churches, journalists, and other countries, has KANU decided to end its political monopoly by repealing Section 2(A) of the *Constitution*, which had made Kenya a one-party state by law. As for the tragedy, the KANU Ministry of Education claimed that anti-government elements are supplying students with drugs and alcohol in order to stir up country-wide strikes. The ministry has not provided any evidence to justify the claim.

To women, the deaths are more—and vivid—proof of the harassment and inequality that women suffer daily. After the tragedy, women's groups set up a permanent committee to examine ways of eliminating discrimination against women. At a memorial service in Nairobi for the nineteen dead girls, the committee read a five-page statement in which it said that murder, rape, defilement, abandonment, harassment, disinheritance, and assault should stop being a painful reality of a woman's life in Kenya. The school, the statement said, is a "mirror of the kind of abuse and violence that women and girls are going through in Kenya—in homes, at the workplace and in public places." Even after the shock expressed over the tragedy, women's groups were pointing out that it was the nineteen dead who were preoccupying the politicians. The multiple rapes and the fact that the crimes were committed by males against females were being overlooked.

My aim in this chapter is to speak to the individual counselor preparing to work with the people of Kenya during this time of turmoil and instability. In doing so, I intend to weave a thread touching upon the search for a Kenyan identity.

The cross-cultural counselor in Kenya straddles two cultures. The home culture (personally speaking, the United States) is familiar; it can, more or less, be taken for granted. Kenya, however, will always to some degree remain unfamiliar. The culture, language, thought pattern, philosophy, and people, however close they become, will always be something "other than" what is native to the counselor.

During the summer of 1983 I was sent as a Maryknoll brother to serve and live among the people and culture of Kenya. The pilgrimage was filled with anxiety, loneliness, detachment, and pain, as well as a sense of awe and wonderment. The initial phase was painful because of the detachment and uprooting from the familiar. It left an emptiness that was to be and has been filled with a new people. In reality, I was naked, for I stripped myself of all that was familiar and now stood before the beautiful culture I was called to embrace. I was a child in every sense of the word. It was a dependency that was to sustain and nurture my every need. I couldn't help but wonder to myself that I was the one who was supposed to "bring something," yet I needed the Kenyan people much more than I ever anticipated. Were they supposed to give to me as well? Learning a new language and entering a new culture is quite a humbling experience if one is willing to trust, submit, and be open to differences of a new people and culture.

So, once again, as the counselor leaves home, there is a tremendous upheaval: emotional, biological, psychological, cultural, spiritual, and functional. What he or she was previously able to take for granted is no longer available. The familiarity of home is no longer. The reality affects every fiber within the counselor's life and system. Edward T. Hall points out tremendous implications for those who plunge into a new home. Stability and predictability, which were so much part of home, are now strangers. Everything humanity is and does is modified by learning and

is therefore malleable. But once learned, these behavior patterns, these habitual responses, these ways of interacting gradually sink below the surface of the mind and like the admiral of a submerged submarine fleet, control from the depths. The hidden controls are usually experienced as though they were innate simply because they are not only ubiquitous but habitual as well (Hall 1977, 42).

As the new counselor travels to Kenya, "the submarine admiral" surfaces to try to discover where the control, the ship, and the sea have gone. He or she is a fish out of water, caught in the middle of unconscious forces: his or her own and also that of the Kenyan, whose awareness of these factors is also below the level of consciousness. The counselor's perception is deeply affected, and these effects are not even known! The disruption that occurs with the initial entry into Kenya, however, can be easily brushed away:

A comment one frequently hears in cross-cultural situations is: "Oh, I just try to be myself and take them as they are. After all, they are adult human beings, aren't they?" Fine and dandy. In superficial social situations, the "be-yourself" formula works. But what if you are an Anglo schoolteacher with a Spanish-American class and are confronted with what appears to be a lack of motivation on the part of your students? You, as a non-Spanish American take it for granted that a certain percentage of children want to do well and to get ahead. So, it comes as a shock when you learn that, to many New Mexican Spanish, to stand out from one's peers is to place oneself in great jeopardy and is to be avoided at all costs. Suddenly, your old stereotypes take on a new meaning (Hall 1977, 42).

The realities of the Kenyan culture that will strike the counselor upon initial entry seem to be novelties, things to be "tried," "admired," and "respected." Yet, he or she may not realize what is perhaps the most important factor of the initial entry into Kenya, namely, the effects of culture on perception. As Hall expressed, these effects are so deeply rooted that they are innate, habitual. The deviation, that is, the entry into Kenya, has not yet disclosed that the person's manner of perception is different, vastly different, from that which is familiar. Thus, to "be oneself" seems the only way to respond at this level of entry.

However, counselors who are exposed initially to the people of the Kenyan culture may wonder if they can be themselves! It is important to note that the manner in which newly arrived counselors perceive their reality is influenced by their expectations; the manner in which they perceive Kenya is influenced by their native cultural reality.

We now turn to one more factor, which adds yet another aspect to this encounter, namely, that to do counseling is a two-way process on the preliminary level of perceiving and being perceived. As the counselor relates and interacts with people, events, and things of the Kenyan culture through the screen of his or her own limited and unique perception, he or she must also remember that the people of Kenya are doing the same.

> In considering the relationships between people and cultures, we tend to regard ourselves as the only ones who make judgments — or at least accurate ones. We must never forget for a moment that other peoples make judgments of us, and that some of them are not too complimentary (Nida 1982).

At this point in the entry into Kenya, therefore, there are many layers of interaction underway, most of which are not at the conscious level of awareness. The counselor's perception of different behaviors within a culturally different climate, cuisine, environment, linguistic, and practical application of his or her vocation contribute to expectations in relation to self and the immediate situation. Something so different on so many levels is unconsciously perceived, to some degree, as comparison.

> Whenever Americans observe graft, unusual sexual behavior, cruelty, an unfamiliar lifestyle, or a different way of planting a crop, they tend to make comparisons on the basis of their conception of American behavior in a similar context. They subsequently arrive at a judgement of good or bad which may mean immoral in one instance or "it doesn't work" in another. The American usually does not take into account the fact that what he or she observes is the behavior of members of

another culture. He or she makes a direct comparison and draws a conclusion from it, whereas a Kenyan for example is likely to say "that is American" rather than "that is bad." Completely oriented to the situation, the Kenyan might judge the context to be inappropriate but would avoid labeling it bad. The implication would be that at the proper place and time it would be appropriate (Stewart 1979, 29).

Perception by the counselor and perception by the Kenyan culture are different in themselves. What is happening at this phase is neither good nor bad; it is, however, different.

I owe a great deal to Lawrence J. Lewis, M.M., who was and is my "spiritual guide from a distance." These past few pages are directly attributed to his work (see Lewis 1984). Indeed, having the past few pages in mind, a good deal is presently being written on psychotherapy from a cross-cultural perspective. Like myself, there are many others who face ethical and skill-related questions about working as a counselor in Kenya or any other overseas milieu. Many others, at times, have experienced firsthand the complete absence of trained professionals in the mental health field, particularly here in Kenya and other third-world countries.

A survey of counsellor-education programs in the U.S.A. revealed that fewer than 1% of the respondents reported any instructional requirements for the study of non-white cultures (Sue 1981, 4).

Also, at a recent conference of psychologists and counselors, a task group recommended that "the provision of professional services to persons of culturally diverse backgrounds (by those) not competent in understanding and providing professional services to such groups . . . be considered unethical" (Sue 1981, viii). As professional counselors, it is our duty to act ethically. To do so as counselors trained in the United States or Europe and functioning in the United States or Europe with clients of similar cultural backgrounds is often difficult. To do so in Kenya, a foreign milieu, or with minority clients of varying levels of inculturation is yet more complicated and demands further preparation and the development of cross-cultural skills. *Competency* is the watchword and achievement of cross-cultural competency is a difficult struggle. For now, let us leave the "how to" till later in the chapter and turn to weaving that thread touching upon the search for a Kenyan identity in hopes that we may better understand those whom we will be counseling.

The search for an African-Kenyan identity begins with Pan-Africanism, a movement which spread out to take different forms. The constant call by African leaders that Africans ought to strive to create a society that respects its cultural values has been heard many times. To be able to do this, Kenyans must first discover themselves. Self-discovery is imperative if they are to be able to venture into the future as a respected people. Kenyans find themselves in a turmoil, and a painful one. They are searching for a future based on their traditions, but one which at the same time is open to changes and to a new world view. The Kenyan of today is a modern person and feels the full impact, if not the blast, of modern civilization. In fact, many Kenyans are torn apart; in a sense, they are falling apart. The sense of being double, a split personality, is felt by many who are influenced by the dualities of: two cultures, two value systems, and two world views — the Kenyan and the Western.

The Pan-African movement sought to find Africans' (Kenyans') roots and to restore the dignity and identity that had been shattered during the slave trade and the colonial period. This movement started at the end of the last century as a spiritual regrouping of leading black people who were conscious of their African origin. In 1905 a group of black intellectuals assembled to organize themselves for defending the civil rights of black people. Pan Africanism initially began, partly, as a reaction against the conditions of racial oppression and exploitation of black Americans. It was a movement for political, economic, civic, and social liberation. This idea of liberation spread to the West Indies and soon found a home among emerging African leaders when the continent was still under colonial rule. Besides West Indian theorists, African leaders like Kwame Nkrumah, Leopold Senghor, Sekou Toure, Jomo Kenyatta (Kenya), and others joined hands to promote the movement toward the government of Africans by Africans.

It is significant to note that most of the leaders destined to conduct Africa to independence grew up in the climate of Pan-Africanism, and Pan-Africanism was recognized as one of the contributing factors toward Africa's independence. After independence, most of these leaders became so involved in the building of their own countries that the idea "we live together" slowly evaporated.

The different movements for promoting African Socialism, African Humanism, Black Consciousness, Negritude, Ujamaa, and so on, definitely have some of their roots in Pan-Africanism. They form part of the inevitable search for an African identity and orientation, which had earlier been emphasized by different African leaders.

Meaningful talk about inculturation, Africanization, or indigenization must and should consider the African identity and world view seriously. History moves on, but we can and must learn from it! African-Kenyan traditions convey certain values, and some of these values could be useful to modern Kenya. Many of the Kenyan traditions are still alive, especially when critical situations arise, for example, sickness and death.

The search for Africa's contribution to world civilization has had a strong impact upon the academic and religious fields. The different disciplines that have cropped up include African history, literature, philosophy, art and theology, to mention just a few that clearly underline the point. The organization of African and Independent churches in Africa is also to be understood within this context.

These and other such attempts need to be understood by the counselor within historical contexts. The pre-independence period in Kenya and other African countries made it necessary to have hopes and aspirations that were, in a sense, expressed in the movements for promoting African Socialism, Negritude, and so on. At stake here is the survival of African-Kenyan values and identities.

The counselor needs to know that some Kenyans are running away from themselves and from their traditional past because of the rapid internalization of some aspects of Western culture. Many Kenyans today believe that the Western value system and world view are of universal validity, which, as such, must be applicable to Kenya. Many do believe that Kenyans can catch up and be like people of the developed countries. Such mental enslavement is the worst side effect of colonialism and of the uninculturated missionary activity. A conscious endeavor is required because "whilst it is necessary for us to tell Westerners to develop a less self-centered view of the world, which inevitably places them in an undue position of superiority, we Africans must struggle to come out of our negative ethnocentrism" (Bengu 1984, art. 2).

As for the above, the counselor and counseling field move out of a colonialist mentality (what is right in the West must be right everywhere) toward a position of dialogue and mutuality. However, many remain ethnocentric or, as David Augsburger names it, "culturally encapsulated" (Augsburger 1986, 22). As counselors, we must fight against this! It is the position of paternalism or "we know best," and it is culturally oppressive. During the period of slave trade, colonialism, and missionary activity, as well as the earlier post-independence era, concepts like "savage," "pagan," "primitive," and "uncivilized" were introduced and used in references, above all, to Africans (Kenyans). Such concepts, even if they might have had neutral connotation or meaning, today are regarded as emotionally loaded and implying value judgment. How can counselors establish a counseling relationship that will avoid this?

First and foremost, the need for appropriate cross-cultural training is needed. The counselor who arrives in Kenya armed only with Western counseling skills, Western theology, and so on, goes forth inadequately prepared. Essential to the task at hand is knowledge of and respect for the religious traditions and cultures of others in Kenya. A theological perspective based on dialogue and realizing God at work in the religions and different cultures of others is primary. Unless we appreciate God enfleshed in all people, true mutuality will not take place in the counseling relationship; rather, it will remain a conversation between the "haves" and "have-nots." Even when I deal with Christians, I must be aware of the bias that "my" history is true salvation while salvation history for "them" began when missionaries arrived and "brought" Christ. The latter perspective devalues the traditions and history of the Kenyan culture.

Second, another essential for counselors arriving in Kenya is some training in anthropological methodology. Without this, Kenya remains a total mystery. Knowledge of systems and dynamics of families very different from our own, of traditional systems in ethnic structures, and of social and cultural realities are all very important tools.

The African continent and Kenya as a country find themselves today in a challenging and critical situation. Pan-Africanism, the OAU, African Socialism, Sensitivity to African Personality, Humanism, Ujamaa, Negritude, Consciencism, and such like, have lost something of their initial pertinence. I believe these movements started from a wrong premise and gave false hopes. The wrong premise was, largely, the idealistic belief in the hope to forge African unity. The myth that African nations could be united must be evaluated. The fact that Kenya fought for independence did not mean it became united. The fact that Kenya suffered under socialism or slavery does not necessarily engender a sense of continental or national solidarity. If there was an identity, it was a transient one, based on the need to unite in fighting the oppressive situation and the particular enemy. Due to individualism, ethnicity, and educational and economic differences, many Kenyans disregard forming a national identity. They happened to be born in Kenya, and some may even wish to have been born elsewhere; however, such wishes have been due to the fact that Kenya is a created state, which uncritically drew inappropriate policies from the Western world. Frantz Fanon was extreme on the issue:

Come Brothers and Sisters, we have too much to do, for us to play the game of a rear-guard. Europe has done what she set out to do, and on the whole, she has done it well; let us stop blaming her, but let us say to her firmly that she should not make such a song and dance about it. We have no more to fear, so let us stop envying her. ... The pretext of catching up must not be used to push humanity around to tear the individual away from him or herself or from his or her privacy, to break and kill him or her (Fanon 1968, 253–54).

Some Kenyans tend to identify themselves with their ethnic group, others with Kenya, a few with the African continent, others with their now formed political party, and still others with "religious belongingness." Many Kenyans get confused when it comes to the question of loyalty. Should one be loyal to the state, to the ethnic group, to the Kenyan traditions, to the family, to a particular form of religion, to modernism, or to oneself?

Who exactly is a Kenyan? The answer to this question differs according to which perspective one wants to underline. Some claim that a Kenyan is a person born in or originating from Kenya, East Africa. Others say it is the color of the skin that distinguishes and identifies the Kenyan. Others trace the links of history to the distant past, including the era of slavery and colonialism. Others see their ethnic and cultural roots: Gikuyu, Luo, Giriama, Masai, and so on.

One thing is sure: an identity of a particular people implies their sharing a culture. The self, the human identity, is a product of socialization and of the culture in which he or she grew up. It is through the process of socialization that a person can internalize a world view, a mode of orientation, and thus acquire a certain identity.

Can one speak of a Kenyan identity or of Kenyan identities? Despite the many different languages, ethnic groups, and distances, there are sufficient affinities and similarities to allow discussion of a Kenyan culture and identity.

The Kenyan identity and world view relies on the community and finds its legitimation in myths and rituals. Africans (and Kenyans), as John Mbiti has noted, are "notoriously religious," and religion permeates all the dimensions of life (Mbiti 1969a, 1).

Just as the Christian world view cannot be separated from the myth of creation (Genesis myth), so also the African world view and identity cannot be separated from African mythology. For instance, the African/Kenyan myths of creation give humankind not only its place in history, but also its identity.

There is no doubt that African/Kenyan myths, especially those about creation, give Kenyans a sense of belonging and of orientation in the local community and society at large. This provides a basis for acceptance, legitimation and stratification of positions in society, in the world, and in "the other world." The other world, the abode of the ancestors, plays a significant role in the traditional Kenyan society.

In Kenyan thinking human beings and nature are animated by the basic principle, a vital force. It is believed that there is no dichotomy between the tangible material world and the invisible whole. In Kenyan traditional life human beings and nature are believed to be bound together. There is a symbiosis.

This symbiosis is not only between humankind and nature, but also between God and human beings. In traditional societies God is seen as the one who organizes and integrates humankind and the world. A similar symbiosis is found between the living and the dead, the ancestors, the latter being taken as custodians of society or as intermediaries between the living and the dead. People's happiness and identity are considered to be influenced by the ancestors, by various spirits, and by the Supreme God.

J. S. Pobee claims that there are three main principles governing the African-Kenyan world view:

(1) The African has a deep religious ontology, which integrally forms a continuum, whereby the living world is incorporated and made dependent upon the spirit world.

(2) The African identity and world view have very strong connections. Whereas the European/American thinks along the line of I think therefore I exist (*cogito ergo sum*), the African says I exist because I belong to a family; I am related by blood, therefore I exist (*cognatus ergo sum*).

Such a *sensus communis* should, however, not be confused with (Marxist) communism.

(3) A human being's sense of finitude, vulnerability, and morality leads many Africans to believe in the power of magic and of super-beings (Pobee 1979, 43–45).

Pobee's claim is important because when we, as counselors, enter into a counseling relationship with a client, and we lack the necessary skills for such an encounter, harm may come about. For example, when entering the counseling relationship with a client from an ethnocentric (*vs.* egocentric) society, movement toward independence and autonomy is harmful. It works toward a "me" mentality for someone functioning in a "we" milieu. Mbiti also draws the following analogy. He says that the culture of the Western individual has encased the person in a protective coat of armor, teaching him or her everything needed to be self-reliant and independent. Yet, behind all this shielding, the Western individual is dying of loneliness. The African-Kenyan individual, on the contrary, is naked before the forces of the world, yet keeps warm by huddling together in a group. Such individuals would die, however, if they ventured outside the group (Mbiti 1969b, 108).

Having touched upon some of the broad aspects of Kenyan people, let us now focus more specifically on cultural characteristics that are especially relevant in pastoral counseling. My aim here is not to be comprehensive, in any sense of the word. Rather, I will present my own experiences of the various phenomena and offer a few pertinent insights.

ANCESTORS

While I was working at the Amani Counselling Society one day, a man in his late thirties came in requesting to "buy" counseling services. We checked the schedule book only to discover that the earliest opening was two weeks off, after the December break. This distressed him greatly because he had hoped to arrange a session before he left on a journey a few days later. As he explained it, he wanted to have a session and talk about a deceased family member so that he (the deceased) would not cause him difficulties during the journey. Finally he agreed to the distant date, saying that he had hoped the deceased relative would understand that he had already made arrangements for him.

Traditionally the ancestors have played a vital and active role in the lives of the living, but their significance has been somewhat suppressed by early missionary opposition and modern scientific education. The emphasis here is on the idea of "belongingness." It is linked with the living-dead (ancestors). The living-dead are still with the family or clan; their process of dying is not yet complete. The counselor must understand that the further the family or clan can go in tracing its origin, the more proud the family; it has found its supporters. The ancestors are regarded as the guardians of the family, and care must be taken to treat them properly.

SPIRIT POSSESSION

One late Friday afternoon, just before closing, two women entered the office and approached the reception area. We exchanged some of the usual greetings, and then the older woman grumbled something. We proceeded into the in-take room, and she broke into a strange language that I presumed was tribal. The younger woman explained, however, "Oh, those are the devils (*mashetani*) speaking." She added that her companion (an aunt) had been possessed for years, and just recently the spirits in her had been demanding to see a doctor. The older woman then threw up her hands and started wild speech. The younger woman brought a bible from her bag, and the older woman settled down. They thanked me and quickly left. I did absolutely nothing except for being present with them a few moments.

Closely akin to Kenyan beliefs in witchcraft (*uchawi*) is the belief in spirit possession. Devil (*shetani*) or spirit possessions are an explanation for a variety of illnesses and misfortunes, particularly barrenness and physical and sexual abnormalities. In a way, spirit possession is a way for the marginal and oppressed to get relief; for example, women who are overworked. Then again, we also see individuals driving a Mercedes Benz to keep an appointment with their witch doctor. Symptoms of possession sometimes include violent shaking, speaking in a strange voice, running wildly, crashing into trees, acting bizarre, tearing off one's clothes, and so on. Once possessed, an individual has a special status in the community.

> Spirit possession occurs because of broken relationships. The exorcism of the demon could not proceed until the problems affecting relationships were resolved. The demons were symptomatic. The cure needed to go behind the symptoms to the detail creating phenomenon which preceded the possession experience (Healy 1981, 85).

It is critical for the counselor to be aware of the culture in many ways. For a widow of the Luo ethnic group to tear off her clothing and jump into the grave of her deceased husband is appropriate behavior. However, what would be the impact of grief counseling if the counselor were unaware of this bit of cultural knowledge?

A woman of the Kuria ethnic group who comes to the counselor and states that she is bothered because "her husband has a rope" is not in fear of being hanged; she is complaining of impotency. The counselor must be willing to go beyond the average level of competency by becoming well versed in nuanced "feeling" words, euphemisms, and idiomatic and slang expressions.

From what has been said, it is clear that the Kenyan world view differs from the Western world view. These two views, which are based on different mentalities, ought to be accepted as being different. Each has a right to exist within its cultural context. However, it is now worth comparing the two views in a short summary.

In the traditional Kenyan concept the individual, family, community, and wider society interpenetrate and form part of the whole. Such is not the case in the Western world view. In the Kenyan concept, the individual is part and parcel of the family, group, community, and society. The individual cannot casually "rub shoulders" with the group; he or she is part of it! In Western thought one can make a clear-cut distinction about how to interact with individuals, family, community, and society.

In the Western view, the individual has a sense of being outside the pressures of the group. In the traditional Kenyan view, on the other hand, the members of the family and extended family significantly interact.

The individual, in order to exist significantly in Kenya, must relate to others. Kinship ties, marriage bonds, initiation ties, covenantal ties, and so on, are there to guarantee that the individual can relate and communicate with others, and thus "be."

From this sense of responsibility by individuals to society and vice-versa comes the need to share. Mutual love, affection, spiritual and material exchange, and sharing in groups form part of the Kenyan identity. Life has more meaning when it is shared with and within the community, family, or group. A sense of solidarity and of being one with others makes one act in a responsible manner.

In the Kenyan moral set-up an individual is expected to be loyal to the group, family, community, society, ancestors, and the Supreme God. The sense of loyalty is bound to the fact that each person forms part of the system.

The concepts of God, religion, and nature vary in Kenya and the West. Western individuals tend to see nature as being down here and God as being up there. The African-Kenyan cosmos includes inanimate, human, and divine dimensions. Nature is not solely there to be defaced, and sometimes debased, by endless scientific and technological conquests (Okolo 1978, 4).

In the Western view, as shown earlier, one is "free," and the relationships one forms are not extensively binding because they do not normally involve as many people as those of the Kenyan. Because of interdependence, Kenyans tend to be more tolerant, flexible, and adaptable.

Does this sound like a perfect society? Indeed, it is not! The vast changes caused by modern development in Kenya are so drastic that one finds it hard to imagine how Kenyans have coped with these changes. Perhaps the strength here is the Kenyan identity, an identity that at times has been ignored and abused, and which is capable of a high degree of adaptability.

So, where do we go from here? Let us now examine the attitude of the cross-cultural pastoral counselor if a helping relationship is to be established here in Kenya. To begin with, counselors need to appreciate themselves as foreigners within Kenya, (as opposed to seeing themselves as wise Westerners in a foreign place) and adopt the perspective of learners. This will be most helpful and beneficial. It is their immediate obligation to immerse themselves in the Kenyan culture and in the language of Ki-Swahili. This is a twofold approach, and neither can be neglected. Only when language skills are finely tuned can counseling begin in earnest.

A second necessary component is finding a cultural informant. A cultural informant is someone in Kenya who will assist the counselor in the process of inculturation. T. P. Harrigan calls this person a "window" into the host culture (Harrigan 1988, 91). It will be helpful, although not essential, if the informant has a knowledge of English and a desire to learn about the counselor's "home" culture.

Recently out of language school in Musoma, Tanzania, with some basic knowledge of Ki-Swahili and the East African culture, I found myself living in Mombasa, Kenya. I met a woman named Mama Maria Sikuku, who not only became my Ki-Swahili tutor but informant as well. Our agreement was that we could speak only Swahili until we reached an impasse (which was quite often, to be truthful). We met three times a week, and all of my cultural questions would be dealt with when I met Mama Sikuku. She showed me the cultural world of Africa through the eyes of a Kenyan, and because of her own curiosity about American culture, I was forced to clarify the how and why of my own American view of various events. With her, I attended important cultural celebrations.

Delving into novels, history, poetry, and drama is exciting, but formal book knowledge is no substitute for firsthand experience of Kenya. It is through a cultural informant that the counselor will begin to see Kenya through the eyes of a Kenyan! This seeking to learn the other's belief system is the foundation of the cross-cultural helping relationship. It is the movement from egocentric identity to other-centric mutuality. This is how one becomes what Augsburger calls an "intercultural" person (Augsburger 1986, 13). The intercultural person is not culture-free, but he or she is also not culture-bound. This belonging-to-both but belonging-to-neither is what T. Olson calls "bifocality" (Olson 1988, 92). Its value cannot be overstated, for from this bifocality flows the ability to view the client as an individual of a culture rather than as a cultural enigma.

In most third-world countries, and most definitely in Kenya, individual supervision is scarce. Small-group supervision and interdisciplinary case seminars, such as the ones I attended during my graduate days at Loyola College in Maryland, are also rare. Ideally, counselors would have a supervisor from Kenya. This is unlikely, however, since the counseling field is just developing here. The only counseling center/institute in all of East Africa is located in Nairobi.

Supervision is a working alliance that focuses on a person's functioning as a counselor; therapy is a working alliance that focuses on one's functioning as a person (Estadt 1983, 53). Reflecting on the impact of Kenya on one's self—preferably through personal therapy—is very much recommended and encouraged. Because of private practice within the Nairobi area, personal therapy is more available than supervision.

A third component which may be worked on prior to the counselor's arrival in Kenya is research. A great deal of cultural research has been done on Kenya and is available both in the United States and Europe. Familiarity with this will enable the counselor to increase his or her knowledge and also to ask the "right" questions. As experience of Kenya (after arrival) confirms or disproves this material, or as new concepts come to light through counseling, the counselor will have an opportunity to add to this body of knowledge and further the field of cultural anthropology as well as cultural psychology.

Finally, a fourth component is cultural relativism. This is the natural outgrowth of healthy cross-cultural attitudes. Cultural relativism admits to the inner cohesion of the Kenyan culture of the clients, allowing them to be understood rather than judged. Three important principles must be taken into account:

1) Contextualization—every bit of behaviour must be considered within the Kenyan framework.

2) Arbitrariness—Kenyans will see the same things differently for no apparent reason.

3) Groundedness—All is grounded in values such as justice, mutual concern, and mutual prizing.

As the counseling process with the East African client begins (in Kenya individuals from Tanzania, Sudan, Ethiopia, Uganda, and elsewhere also seek out services), evaluation and assessment involves the same four sequential steps that would be followed in a same-culture setting, but with nuanced differences related to the client's culture (Weiner 1975, 51).

STEP 1: IDENTIFYING THE PRESENTING PROBLEM

For example, if it is not clear why the particular issue presented is a problem, the counselor must rely on the primary axiom of cross-cultural counseling—*never* pretend to understand! If the client's presenting problem does not make sense, it is imperative that the counselor say so. This not only clarifies the problem, but establishes a precedent for honesty. This must be reinforced in the first session by informing your client that because you are from another culture, there may be times when you do not understand.

STEP 2: EXPLORING THE BACKGROUND OF THE PROBLEM(S)

This flows naturally from the first step, keeping in mind how short term counseling is here. However, the counselor need not be too rushed or afraid to ask such a question as, "How does that usually work in your ethnic group?" As mentioned earlier in the chapter, when dealing with a Kenyan client, the counselor is also involved with his or her extended family, which is a powerful therapeutic institution and brings along the sense of community.

STEP 3: UNDERSTANDING THE CLIENT AS A PERSON

Much of the chapter is just on this point. Many clients suffer from a lack of resources and opportunities. I had always assumed, before arriving in Kenya, that counseling was only useful once one's basic needs had been met, but I no longer think that. The counselor's interest and attention can indeed enhance the client's self-worth and enable the person to see opportunities not seen before.

STEP 4: ARRIVING AT A WORKING DIAGNOSIS

The first three steps should lead to a tentative diagnosis, from which treatment can begin. To repeat, it is important to know cultural norms and customs as a background to any diagnostic formulation.

Assessing the client involves motivation, ability, and functioning (Weiner 1975, 61). In general, Kenyans who present themselves for counseling have either exhausted the culturally normative systems or find them not available. This indicates that distress is somewhat acute and motivation high. However, counselors must be on guard against seekers of magical cures! The client's ability to reflect and talk about himself or herself can usually be determined in the initial interview. The counselor, however, must guard against rapid-fire questioning. Patience will allow the client to elaborate. He or she, after all, is in a foreign environment, the office of an expatriate profession, just as the counselor is in a foreign environment.

Finally, in assessing appropriateness of a client for therapy, counselors need insight into the client's present functioning or personality integration. This is best obtained by asking simple, open-ended questions about areas of their life which may or may not be related to the presenting problem or problems. By listening carefully and assessing day-to-day functioning, the counselor should have some idea of the client's ability to function in therapy.

As I opened up the chapter, I will now close by stating that the agenda on the minds of Kenyans these days is change. Kenya is a country where a very beautiful people are at a crossroads. Cross-cultural counselors *can* make a difference in lives. There are those times when God calls us to move into unfamiliar waters, whether in ministry, location, or calling. The journey will have dark nights as well as joy-filled experiences. Time in Kenya offers variety, different directions, unique individuals, and the ordinary of everyday life.

4

Malawi

DORIS GASTONGUAY

Sister Doris Gastonguay writes of her many-faceted ministry as a pastoral counselor in Malawi, South Africa. In welcoming the reader to the soil of her adopted homeland, Sister Doris paints a picture of the Malawi cultural landscape and then leads us into her personal journey as a pastoral counselor within the context of the Malawi culture, where traditional practices and expectations cross over with modern urban life.

"It is not Western, it is not village," Sister Doris comments. "It is an ability to shift back and forth from one world to the other."

As I was considering the feasibility of writing this chapter, an unusually clear and vivid dream came to me in the early morning hours.

Two men who have been very significant in my life came to me, each with a gift. The first person has not been seen or heard of for a good fifteen years. He brought me a new book entitled *Simon Sighs.* This book had been talked about (in my dream world) and was supposed to be of awesome content. It was given for my personal refreshment. The second person, a kindred spirit and spiritual companion for a good twenty years, but also absent and not seen for five, had scheduled an hour for me. He handed me small slips of paper with scripture quotations. It was difficult to speak privately because of other persons invading our space.

The dream excited me. It referred to a worthy book of rich content, and it told me the exercise would refresh me. I must bring to the fore the

46

scriptures, which underlie and support all I believe and pass on. I hardly needed reminding that the quiet time and private space needed for such an exercise are rare. Without this dream I probably would not have pursued the project. Malawians, too, respect their dreams, and dream work has created openings into counseling.

Counseling rests on the reality of the human person, each one's life journey and quest, situated in time and space. As I consider the mystery of *personhood,* the suffering that is implied in *growth,* and the possible significance of pastoral counseling fostering *life,* a word comes to my mind: *holistic.*

Any avenue into — or coming from — the psyche may have some relevance and must be taken into consideration as we seek health, wholeness, and holiness. Our sense perceptions of the body before us give initial data; the human sciences expand our understanding; and a scripture-based theology opens to the immortal and the Infinite. A holistic approach that integrates all this, incorporating the cultural contrasts that are our focus here, or at least attempts to do so, is essential to any understanding of the human person in whatever phase of becoming the present moment finds him or her.

Part 1 will look at the human person, the direction of life, and some cornerstones for pastoral counseling. Part 2 will introduce Malawi . . . welcome! Part 3 moves into the very core of my counseling experience here. Part 4 provides some evaluation; we step back, size it up, and look ahead.

PART 1: ABOUT THE HUMAN PERSON, THE DIRECTION OF LIFE, AND SOME CORNERSTONES FOR PASTORAL COUNSELING

THE WONDER OF MY BEING

We come from God and carry God's likeness. We are shaped according to the divine purpose.

Let us make man to our image and likeness (Genesis 1:26).
You formed me in my inmost being (Psalm 139:13-14).
The potter was working at the wheel (Jeremiah 18:3-4).

I see the dignity of this image stamped on the features of even the most simple, unsophisticated village woman I meet as I walk Malawi's garden paths and meet her peoples. God sustains each of us with a continuous and loving concern, through an intimate awareness of everything that touches us.

What am I that you care for me, keep me in mind (Psalm 8).
My words are known to you even before I speak them (Psalm 139:4).

We speak of Africans as being naturally religious. They do seem to live in daily contact with higher powers and invisible worlds. The nature of our relationship to God will doubtlessly remain the most amazing reality I shall ever have to contend with.

The Spirit of God is upon me (Isaiah 61:1; Luke 4:18).
The Spirit of God dwells within you (Romans 8:9).
We will come and make our home in him (John 14:23).

There are beautiful African legends of the first man's dialogue with God, who communicated through the swaying of the banana tree leaves.

I easily read this faith vision of the human person in the teachings of Carl Jung, contemporary psychologist (1875-1961). My capacity to know God will surely be in some proportion to my conscious awareness of life around me—both the visible and the invisible. God's fashioning of my inmost being moves me down into my unconscious levels, both personal and collective. Archetypes therein contain the very images of God—which I am invited to manifest through my outer persona. Christian warfare contains the confrontation and taming of inner shadow elements; and where better for an animus projection to go than onto Jesus the Lord himself!

Of what relevance is all this to my *Malawi world*? It all applies as well to

- the beggar at the door asking for food ...
- the woman whose husband just died of AIDS, who feels the symptoms coming on in her body, and who will leave eight children unprovided for ...
- the refugees who have crossed our borders seeking asylum from the violence devastating their homeland, nearly one million of them ...

I speak equally of
- the wonderfully dedicated lay persons who give their weekends and holidays to retreat work "all for the Kingdom," and whose hunger for more of God is never satisfied.
- the dynamic life-giving women religious whom we (of the Western world) have led into collective molds and who now cry (as indeed we did) for some of that fresh air announced by Good Pope John ...

The immediate needs appear to be socio-economic,
while the deeper are for *recognition as persons,*
so "wonderful in their being"—
and this is guaranteed to cross any cultural barriers.

THE MYSTERY OF GROWTH AND BECOMING

St. Paul does not seem to understand himself, and we know the feeling: "Indeed I do, not the good I want, but the evil I do not want" (Romans 7:15ff).

The process of growth is very laborious as "All creation groans, and we too groan inwardly as we await the redemption of our bodies" (Romans 8:22-23). The rites of passage within African cultures, which initiated into a new stage of life, often tested the endurance of the initiate. The secrecy that enveloped them produced that very lack of understanding described by St. Paul.

To human beings alone is given freedom of choice, which is founded on a discerning awareness of good/evil: "Test everything. Follow the good, avoid the evil" (1 Thessalonians 5:19). The criteria for good and evil vary from one culture to another. Freedom of choice, as I have observed it here, is so conditioned by peer pressures and the "powers that be" that our very definitions will differ.

The scriptures likewise knew that there was more to us than a simple outer persona or even the conscious ego. "May your hidden self grow strong" (Ephesians 3:16). Developmental psychology teaches us that the adolescent crossing into young adulthood must not only develop ego autonomy but respect what his or her deeper self wants to become. The midlifer will wrestle until unconscious shadows are tamed, and the "I" kneels to the One within. In later years, after forty years of marriage, the requirements of love will be at the same inner depths of surrender and no less a challenge.

Developing and maintaining an appropriate outer persona often consumes so much of the energies of the persons I encounter here that the real inner self may suffer long and major eclipses ... but what treasures lie within, an even greater challenge to counseling skills.

INTEGRATION AND FULLNESS OF LIFE (PSYCHOSYNTHESIS)

The ultimate goal of our becoming is clearly stated in Ephesians 1:4-10, where all is to be brought "into unity under Christ—according to the Father's mysterious purpose." "Peoples, tribes, tongues, nations will truly serve him" (Daniel 7:13-14) only when all that is within me bends the knee proclaiming the Lordship of Jesus (Philippians 2:11). On that day the fullness of shalom promised in the Hebrew Scriptures (Isaiah 11:6, Hosea 12:20—"I will banish warfare from the country") becomes the fullness of Life as promised by Jesus in John 10:10.

Integration of all my faculties will find a new serenity in this at-one-ness, and maybe I will have that sense of homecoming at journey's end. I have often come face to face here in Malawi with older, wiser persons of the most simple background who do carry that stamp of being at home in themselves. It leaves me in awe.

SOME PASTORAL COUNSELING CORNERSTONES

Ten years ago almost to the day (June 1981) I sat before my thesis faculty examination board composed of Barry Estadt, Mel Blanchette, and Jack

Compton, who have each in turn occupied the director's chair for the Loyola pastoral counseling program.

First, I held a camera in my hand and used it, signifying that I was attending to what was observably present. Step two consisted in retelling my myth story of each of these persons, speaking of *relationships* that fostered a specific kind of growth in my initiation to pastoral counseling. Third, I wore a bright African Java print dress; *Malawi* would be the space where Loyola seeds would be planted.

The thesis I presented and defended was an articulation of what I most believe in and still operate from. Let us speak of counseling cornerstones. Pastoral counseling is a *relationship* that is in constant dynamic tension as two persons journey together. This relationship requires initial *trust* between the two persons concerned. A taming process then ensues; a contract must be established; a fidelity to regular presence be maintained; a perseverance through resistances, projections, and so on is required; and finally, there is the terminal weaning and leave-taking ... with the door remaining open for whatever follow-up encounters may prove helpful. Initiating a cross-cultural pastoral counseling relationship is far more complex than one with "someone like me."

Pastoral counseling is a *faith in life*. I continue to believe and reaffirm that the person before me is entrusted with a spark of life. I witness that the spark has its own intrinsic power to become a living flame. The spark at times gets buried under dead coals and needs to be freed, but always the life force is there. Each person is entrusted with a unique goodness, a precious gift, which wants to grow to its full potential, all according to an in-built pattern. The environment strongly affects growth. Strength for the journey, solutions to problems, hopes in times of darkness, are *within the person.* This means that *my* values, *my* convictions, *my* ways of doing, *my* answers may be absolutely useless and meaningless for the person before me. The pastoral counseling relationship has a goal to *release* that which is within the other. Only if it serves this purpose will my own life experience, enriched by Loyola training, be of some use. Cross-cultural counseling necessitates a passage through all the surface appearances and differences, which can be deceiving. The drums we dance to *do* beat a different rhythm, but dance we must, for such is life, and maybe somewhere in the dance we will touch our common human heritage.

I am by nature a messenger of joy. I want everyone to live happily and harmoniously together. I used to turn away when people began tales of woe; I would change the subject when conversations got too heavy. The world's sufferings and tragedies were just too much; I felt so utterly helpless in the face of it all. "God, what a mess!" Loyola formation operated an extraordinary inner conversion within me, enabling me to be with those in need. Empathy is the key. The smile and the caring attentive heart quickly cross cultural barriers.

Life is one.

The *spiritual* journey (Ignatian Exercises, John of the Cross), the *psychological* unfolding (Jung, Erikson, Levinson), and *physical* growth (child, adolescent, young adult, mid-lifer, senior) are parallel and interconnected. A single event at any level has consequences for the whole person. Life-stopping events often open doors to a new level of being. The body does not lie, and sleep-dreams tell the truth. Nothing may be ignored without penalty.

Know and situate others in their life journey, at all levels. Have they accomplished the developmental tasks of the psyche that are appropriate for and expected at certain stages? Have they a God to walk with and to worship? Are there physical obstacles to cherished dreams?

Draw out from others the story-myth they tell themselves albeit unconsciously: Where do I come from (Genesis)? What are major forces affecting my life (Incarnation)? What is my present dilemma (Crucifixion for Redemption)? What kind of heaven do I dream of (Eschatology)? This will put them in conscious communion with their inner energies and where their life wants to go. It will create new spaces for new life to emerge.

I believe what I have just said is true regardless of culture. Perceptions and formulations, however, widely differ. Western culture makes much of the body-mind-soul trilogy, while I doubt that my friends here are much concerned. They would find it much more relevant to speak of self in relation to others, God, and nature. They understand that the individual is perpetuated and living in the ancestral blood line, which has very important consequences.

I remember inviting a Malawian, Ph.D., priest-friend to comment on my presentation of Jungian concept of the psyche. His outline was so completely different that I could not believe we were addressing the same subject. I have revised my thinking; we have *much* to learn from each other. Westerners are still trying to recover from the Descartes split of body and soul by preaching a holistic approach. Such an approach is probably quite natural to my friends here.

PART 2: WELCOME TO MALAWI, THE WARM HEART OF AFRICA

This catch phrase was adopted by the Department of Tourism, and it aptly describes the human climate of the country. Malawi is a small land-locked country extending some seven hundred miles from north to south. It is greatly influenced by its beautiful lake, 350 miles long by fifty miles at its widest point, a veritable inland sea. There are highlands where temperate fruit may be grown, and there are savanna tall-grass and umbrella tree spaces where elephants and lions used to roam. There are lower lands bordering the lake, or the Shire River outlet into the south, uncomfortably hot with the tropical sun at its most powerful. The people are delightfully human, fully alive; they give true respect to those whose intentions are honest. They have suffered colonialism and worked their way out of it under charismatic leadership. They are desperately hungry for the "moreness" of life, which combines the good things of God's creation with the abundance of life promised in the gospels. I arrived in 1957 as a young sister, and I have spent most of my working years here. Each return has been a home-coming.

SOME CULTURAL DOMINANTS

Love of life. Love of life is certainly most deeply rooted. To be life-bearing and nurturing is so ingrained that it overrules any other norms. Joy is spontaneous. I know of no other people who laugh so easily. Even in the midst of trouble, a smile will flash in response to any sympathetic enquiry. Life is the greatest of gifts, and simple everyday things are reviewed with gratitude.

Hospitality. For Malawians hospitality is a must. A visitor is never turned away or allowed to leave without some offer of food. They give the best of whatever is on hand, even if it means they themselves must do without. In village visits in the early years we would cycle back home with some eggs in our apron pockets, or some beans, or a few maize cobs—all received from families where basic sustenance is never taken for granted. Today Malawi's population of eight million hosts nearly one million Mozambican refugees; Malawians could never hoard food while others went without.

Languages. Banthu languages all have a similar grammatical structure. The wisdom of the ages is contained in richly imaged proverbs that teach the facts of life. *Kupatsa nkuika*: you are expected to give, because what you give will come back to you. *Walira mbvula, walira matope*: If you have cried for rain, you have equally invited the mud. *Zapita, zapita; dazi lilibe mankhwala*: It is gone, baldness has no remedy; you cannot recapture the past. Chichewa is the national language, used widely in the Central and Southern regions. English serves as international code.

Family. The extended family is of such importance that it permeates all of life. In the matrilineal tribes mainly in the Central and Southern regions, the firstborn son is responsible for his sisters and their children. His own children are accountable to the senior uncle on their mother's side. The firstborn daughter at age five or six might be given over to the maternal grandmother to help her carry water, firewood, and so on. Our notions of family counseling *really* need rethinking. How does one have a family ses-sion with the whole of the extended family present? Yet, in fact, there are few private quarrels. Cases are resolved publicly with advisors and all con-cerned present and speaking their minds. Marriage seems not to be between two individuals as much as a marrying into another extended family. Maybe family counseling would come more naturally in such a setting, where there is such a need to be together.

The complexities of intertribal marriages seem endless. In the north of Malawi, where a patrilineal tribe dominates, a dowry bride-price is given to the girl's family. She is then received into the husband's family. The children belong to his side. If for some reason the marriage does not work, to return her to her family would necessitate the return of the dowry, which of course has been consumed in the interim. In the matrilineal set-up, the young man must prove himself a hard worker and a good provider in the eyes of the in-laws, build a house beside the mother-in-law, and "fit in."

Obviously, an expatriate counselor could *never* just walk in and advertise services. There is a need to become acquainted with "what is done" and "what is not done," and "who" is "who" for the other. When a student announces that her brother is visiting her, the counselor must check out *which* brother: the blood brother of the same mother's womb, the cousin, the village neighbor, the student from the Boys' School, the intended fiancé, or just plain lover! All may be termed brother.

Age. Age opens one to wisdom and commands respect. Growing older in Malawi brings certain compensations. I might regret my loss of a certain physical fitness, long treks on bicycle, stamina to push myself on. Accompanying these diminishments, however, I have experienced increased attention given to what I share from my own life experience. A new relation to others has developed. From being simply a sister, or even spiritual mother, it is the archetypal *wise woman* now being called forth in a way that my own country of origin surely ignores. In the traditional set-up, the number of years goes a long way in establishing seniority. The streak of gray in my hair suddenly brought new credibility—I love it!

Time. Time is not measured by the clock. I think my Afro-Malawian friends can much more readily understand the difference between kairos and chronos events. Western minds have a linear concept of time, from one date to another, where minutes, hours, and days are counted off. Kairos timing is the *event* itself. It concerns the people involved and directs attention to whatever their needs and concerns are at that moment. "How much *time* will I need to visit my daughter? The time it will take to meet each other. She will give me a return bus ticket home when the time of my visit is finished." Note that the host must provide return fare!

Death. It is essential to cry at the funeral (literally *"Kulira maliro"*). I buried my younger sister a few years ago, and I do not even remember my tears at the time. I returned to Malawi a few months after, and friends came to offer condolences. They knelt in a circle and started singing. The funeral songs are the most expressive. It was *then* that my inner reservoirs broke. People leave work and lose pay to attend a funeral. Everything stops.

On a recent Sunday, one of our sisters involved in a nearby parish had a full day of meetings scheduled. She arrived to find that there had been two tragic deaths. The agenda of the day was neatly brushed aside, and people divided themselves into two groups to "be with" the families in sorrow. The casket is never left alone for a single moment, and tears mingle with prayer and songs. The tragic drama of death is fully honored even while Christian hope is shared. These are profound psychological necessities, which our technological societies have brushed aside.

SIGNIFICANT CULTURAL FACTORS DIRECTLY INFLUENCING COUNSELING

Traditional Advisors ("*Alangizi*"). Education—socialization of the child into family and village life—was traditionally through peer group initiations, conducted by officially appointed advisors. Girls of a same age were taught the same patterns of behavior and introduced to new skills together. They were later prepared for marriage, motherhood, and adult responsibilities, all according to a tightly structured code of behavior, always with a designated advisor. Individuals expected to be told what to do, how to behave. The advisor would become a senior friend and companion, a mentor, as it were, for those times. The aim was much more to transmit a traditional truth than to develop the person according to who or what each could become.

With the advent of boarding school education, urbanization, and inter-tribal marriages, much of the old has been lost without a comparable replacement. Western materialism, capitalistic competition and consumerism, and achievement ambitions have all been counter-cultural and often devastating in their effects.

There is space and real need for a new generation advisor, a counselor. The *Alangizi* had an important traditional role, laying a foundation upon which a sensitive pastoral counselor can build.

Power of the Peer Group. Conformity to group norms is a very early lesson required of any member of these societies. There is no place for deviance however justifiable it might be in Western eyes. Who would *dare* to be different? Value is placed on remaining inconspicuous among equals. Special giftedness must be disguised. Any kind of superiority (physical or mental) must be masked under the most modest and humble exterior. A certain passivity is developed in the classroom, lest jealousies be aroused by praise from the teacher.

I knew that setting up an office with regular office hours and expecting clients to walk in for individual counseling would be a joke. The result would have been many solitary waiting hours!

Secrets and privacy are immediately suspect in the eyes of the collectivity. A word spoken is immediately public information. What kind of counseling is needed, and how to initiate it, are good questions.

Collective Responsibility. There are many classical stories about powerful chiefs who commanded immense tribes. The secret? Before making any public statements, or giving orders that would mobilize many, they would always ensure the support of the advisors or elders surrounding them. They sounded out public opinion in advance. Then the leader could stand and command.

Much of our counseling seeks to awaken a personal sense of responsibility for personal needs and decisions. Traditionally, individual responsibility comes in only where there is a specifically assigned task within a communal project. For the unforeseen, the call for spontaneous involvement, there is easily a shrug of the shoulders with a *"Zao"* — meaning, that is not my concern but "theirs," whoever that might be.

This mentality has certainly been carried over into imported institutions. Schools and convents easily carry what to Westerners would be culpable passivity. "Somebody" should have done it, but nobody did. Work evenly shared will most likely be done, and the one who would drag behind is quickly made to tow the line. Anything else can be equated to showing off or putting oneself forward; such behavior is to be avoided at all costs.

Along the same line of thinking, there is a wide gap between cultures in the understanding of evil, what constitutes it, and how it affects our lives. I have often heard the "cannot do otherwise" inherent in some statements. A man has taken a second wife: "It is the time for it" (*nthawi yake yafika*). Having said that, no further considerations are expected. A vowed celibate has fathered a child: "It was the time for it." A young girl has the physical maturity to bear children, but no marriage is in sight; the signals are given that she is available ... life must be perpetuated. What would be deviant sexual behavior for the Western mind may have an entirely different context here.

The non-judgmental attitude of the counselor will be mightily challenged.

A Culture in Transition. Malawi, like its neighboring countries, has experienced fast-moving changes in all spheres of life: political, economical, social, and religious. Much of the population has remained rural, yet even these settings have been affected by the technologies, materialism, and individualism of the modern world.

Traditional values have lost much of their raison d'etre, yet are seen to coexist with their exact opposites. Kneeling is still practiced as a sign of respect by students to teacher, wives to husbands, religious sisters to their community superiors—however sophisticated they may have become as individuals. Inadequate wages seem to be accepted, continuing the spirit of the free labor a villager "owed" his chief for protection. In times of crisis many city dwellers are drawn back to the village for prescribed rites of healing, purification, and reconciliation.

Students are no longer held by village taboos within the school compounds, but remain connected with the same fears that produced them. They must at the same time satisfy their village grandmother with her mores, and the requisites of simple survival in the modern jungle of clothes, money, sex, and social recognition. A student subculture has evolved as a coping mechanism.

Women religious, receiving little or no personal ongoing formation after final vows, are now showing all the signs of modern pressures: migraines, high blood pressure, peptic ulcers.

In and through all this, I truly believe a strong instinctive conservation based on traditions of the past has been relegated to the collective unconscious of all who profess exteriorly the freedom to live as they choose. In a moment of crisis the old ways surface. We are dealing with *both* the old and the new.

Would you believe that most of these people do not even know that pastoral counselors exist and that they might be helpful. The task at hand is a new job description, for a new kind of counselor, who will respond to real life needs in a manner that is socially acceptable. It is a significant challenge!

PART 3: THE PASTORAL COUNSELING EXPERIENCE

THE EXPERIENCE OF THE PASTORAL COUNSELOR

I remain convinced that:
- life is a tremendous gift as well as a most serious responsibility;
- there is a God of gods, who gifts us, invites us, draws us to fullness of life;
- all are gifted and called and destined to that fullness;
- my own fears and pain are an integral part of the human becoming, and so are the fears and pains of others;
- just as wise, understanding, and respectful others have enabled me to overcome obstacles and grow, so I can, in turn, help others.

Counseling implies my commitment: to be with the other; to become as a mirror so that he may see and find himself; to so journey with her that she knows she is no longer alone, and even after the parting of ways will never walk alone; to enflesh the fidelity that renews the client's trust and faith in humankind; to searching with others that they might find their own answers.

I will *not* walk for others where they should go. I will not decide for them their course of action; I will not speak for them where they must learn the art for themselves. I will not do the task which they must master on their own. But I will be there, all theirs, with an ear they can chew off, with all the attention I can muster. This is because I care and I want others to live. Yes, more than anything, I want others to live, to find the joy and happiness they were created for. I want them to become the person that wants to grow out of them, to know the freedom of the children of a God who loves unconditionally and who indeed will be with us always.

MINISTRY IN THE SCHOOL CONTEXT

I left Loyola, returning to Malawi in 1981, assigned to religious education (R.E.) in post-primary schools. The intense year at Loyola, with a practicum at Howard University Counseling Service, was done with the immediate intention of applying the skills as appropriate and according to possibility among school youth.

Instead of setting up an office with hours, I simply told my first R.E. class of thirty Catholic students in the second year of high school that I wanted to get to know them better. I suggested that I would call them in alphabetical order for a short "chat." I tendered the invitation in a warm friendly manner, but was very direct about it! It was important to use the same basic topics with each one, because I knew they would compare notes: family, health, hobbies and interests, boy friends, career aspirations. They loved it! The personal attention was, first of all, a novelty—the norm was five hundred students cramped into space for 360, with fifty to sixty in classrooms meant for thirty, heavy teaching schedules for teachers with pressure of external exams, and so on. In such conditions individual counseling takes on the quality of a luxury. Out of the initial contact, some came back for more. That's how it all began.

My next step was to begin prayer meetings over the lunch hour break: "Come with a Song, a Psalm, a Prayer." This created an opening for students of other religious denominations. I also told them they could come on Saturday mornings if they wanted to see me for more personal prayer intentions. That approach also proved to be acceptable and was another beginning.

The Psychology Club followed. This had great appeal because it had a college flavor to it. Twelve students showed up, and when others saw them doing the Myers-Briggs Typology Inventory (MBTI) and the Edwards (EPPS) questionnaires, my intake doubled. Each week I introduced a new topic, and this led to individual encounters for more serious reflection on personality and behavior. Time can be a problem in boarding schools because students are tightly scheduled to keep them out of mischief, but we managed. The Edwards PPS, which gives a ranking order of basic needs or drives, beautifully complements the MBTI typology.

I can smile now at the modest beginnings. I saw two students in a row who were strongly introvert (confirmed in the classroom) with a surprisingly high percentile for aggression—*not* visible. The interview went something like this:

Counselor:	Do you get angry sometimes?
Student:	Oh yes!
Counselor:	What do you do when you are angry?

Student:	I hold it in and wait till it goes away.
Counselor:	How do you feel during this time? Any physical reaction?
Student:	(Reflectively) Sometimes I get a headache.
Counselor:	Do you think there is any connection between anger and the headache?
Student:	(Puzzled)
Student:	What would happen if you found a safe way of getting the anger out?
Student:	Can I do that?
Counselor:	See what happens if you go jogging around the sports field. Or go to your next manual work assignment telling your anger to go into the hoe or the grass slasher.
Student:	(Surprised) I can do that?
Counselor:	Try it. Oh, and another thing, do you have a friend you can trust?
Student:	Yes.
Counselor:	Then tell her you need to talk about being angry. Tell her what has made you angry, and how you feel about it. She does not need to do or say anything—just listen and be with you. This is another way of getting the anger out. If you keep it in, it will surely make you sick. Can you do this?
Student:	Oh yes!
Counselor:	Let me know if you get another headache.

The student following her had the same heading of introverted aggression. Our encounter followed a similar pattern, except that she found anger upset her stomach. When I asked her if she had a friend to whom she could talk, the reply was, "Yes, the girl who was just here with you, before me." I wondered afterward if they had answered the questionnaires together! Oh well, it has to begin somewhere.

Unfortunately, after only the first term, I was sent to other schools and started giving weekend (team) retreats. This meant that I was not in one place long enough to permit longer-term relationships. I used the same pattern of time given to individuals following an R.E. class period, and some serious clients emerged. Vocation discernment had some beautiful results, for example, a teacher training college student is scheduled for ordination next year as a result of counseling discernment.

WORKSHOP APPROACH, WOMEN RELIGIOUS

Shortly after my return to Malawi in 1981, I was invited to contribute to a renewal program for women religious. The area entrusted to me was psychology of personality under the informal heading of "Know Yourself." I had had a privileged experience of group spiritual direction in the late

'70s, where we started with input of psychological realities. The use of personality questionnaires and tools such as dream work prepared us to share our faith journey in a much more holistic way. William Jerema (Loyola M.Sc.) had taken the initiative of bringing this group together. With "all" my counseling training, I remain at heart a teacher. When something delights me, when truth out there resonates with the deeper wisdom within, when something "works" then my instincts are to share the good news. I have experienced that the teaching leads into the counseling: "Come and see me to talk about what all this means to you." We quickly move into psychic depths because of the nature of the material. From: "I am like this" to "I don't like to be like this" to "It hurts" to "I am really crying inside" to "How can I go on living this?" The pastoral counseling relationship is naturally called forth.

From that first 1982 session I became a regular resource person for Ongoing Formation workshops sponsored by the Association of Women Religious of Malawi (ARIMA). This association brings together the major superiors of some twenty-three religious congregations, representing about seven hundred sisters, of whom almost five hundred are Malawian. The four local congregations have no direct contacts to outside sources of religious renewal, and I really hear their cry for "more life."

In 1983 and again in 1985 I teamed up with a priest, again at the invitation of ARIMA, for a three-week seminar looking at religious life and personality integration. Shorter sessions were spread over the school holidays. I was still doing R.E. during weekdays and student retreats on weekends, so it was not surprising that I went home in 1986 a near burn-out case. I think most of us have to go through a phase of balancing what we give out with how we renew our energies. I spent nine months in the United States letting go, collapsing, and slowly building up. I did not even have the energy to get myself out to Loyola in Columbia—I really missed that.

Returning in 1987 I gradually diminished the school involvement and now give full-time to both men and women religious, formation houses, and individual congregations. The Jesuit thrust of promoting spiritual psychology has been invaluable. A topic like the Enneagram opens to new consciousness and new responsibility. The personal encounter flowing from materials presented calls forth all the skills I have developed.

I initially felt that there was so much knowledge to impart that I overloaded the input part of the workshops. I have gradually come to see that giving time and space for a simple personal encounter is where the real action is and where I put to use all of my Loyola training. I may see someone only twice in the course of a week, but we go to depths that would take weeks of counseling sessions to reach.

The high spot of any workshop-counseling situation for me is when I see the "aha!" look come into a person's eyes. They see, are amazed at what they see, and seem to experience new energies from the very seeing.

I was giving a two-week workshop to doctrinal students, sisters preparing for final vows, coming from three African countries. I used picture projections to help them begin to find images to describe themselves. One had chosen a newly built home, where two men were on the roof finishing up. She was describing her house:

Client: It is a new house. It is big and much too nice for me.
Counselor: So you have built yourself a new house during these months?
Client: What?
Counselor: You are going home a new person. That is what the picture is saying.
Client: Oh! ... (this was the moment of revelation. There was silence as this registered consciously.)
Counselor: You have new walls, new roof, and new spaces inside.
Client: (Pause and then) Yes! Yes, I have. It is true. I *am* different.
Counselor: Shall we visit the rooms? Show me what you see.

And from there we saw the spacious sitting room, with a big hearth; a chapel, which had new meaning as a private space to meet God. She entered into the game, visibly taken up by it.

At the end of such a workshop, I am credited with having helped them come home to themselves, of finding new ways of understanding self and others, new ways of relating, and even of finding God as never before. This is what Loyola has enabled me to do *in and through* cultural diversity.

DREAM WORK

My tale would be incomplete without a reference to dream work. I have been writing my dreams since an initial introduction to the Intensive Journal in 1974. It was eventually through our experience of group spiritual direction that I became more conscious of the power underlying dream images. Learning one's inner symbolic language takes time, but over the years the efforts bear fruit. To this day I am amazed at how sharply and clearly my dreams reveal myself to me.

Dream work has found fertile soil among my Banthu African friends. In this world dreams are taken seriously. People believe in their dreams, attribute prophetic powers to them, and act upon them. I cannot remember a single dream workshop where there has not been at least one person telling me that when he or she dreams of death, it happens. The invitation to look into their dreams immediately opens doors. There is a natural curiosity and an innate sense of the dream's value.

What is new for them is the symbolic dimension. From a simple literal interpretation (which must in any case be checked out), we move to the relational content (the dream may be telling me something about how I actually feel toward a certain person). Finally, there is the intra-psychic level, where all parts of the dream relate to my inner world and contain an existential message for my own life. A dream about my older sister, who "always knew everything," has nothing to do with her now, but rather contains wisdom for my own life.

One sister described the following dream:

> I was walking along the road when it became very muddy. It was very hard to walk, and I found it tough going. Then, I found I was walking in a kind of foam, like the soap makes. It was delightful! My feet hardly touched the ground and I could just float along. Then I came to a garden and started picking flowers.

The dream could belong to any culture. It was an easy step into reflecting on what was very difficult and trying for her in that period of her life. Likewise, there were new experiences of grace. The flowers plucked were easily identified as the flowers she liked to "pick for Jesus" in the simplicity and generosity of her own daily life.

A good example of moving from the literal to the symbolic came during a three-week program. I had given the basic outline of dreams, nature of, how to work with, and so on. At the end of two weeks we had planned a pilgrimage to a waterfall some two miles distant. That morning a sister awaited me at the dining room door. "Sister, I had a dream. We must not go into the forest." I heard her out over breakfast. The dream went like this:

> We were walking through the forest. You were in front, and Fr. N. was bringing up the rear. Suddenly a big lion came roaring down toward us. You ran away and Fr. N. was eaten up.

She continued, almost pleading, "If someone had had that dream in the village, no one would go to the forest that day." I invited her to feel very free about participating in the morning's outing; we would pray for protection before departure and proceed as planned. She came with us. It was a lovely trek with a variety of prayer experiences on the way. There were no mishaps.

Returning to base, I invited her to sit with me for lunch. No lions? She was a bit shy. "Now, my friend, what is all this about lion power inside you? I have been leading you into the forest of your unconscious. Fr. N. has been reflecting with you on your religious life. By next week we will have dispersed; I will have 'run away.' The dream is saying the lion power may devour your religious life. Shall we look at that lion inside you?" She burst out laughing—the "Aha" connection. The "lion" was very visible in the stout matronly authoritative woman, and yes, the lion could get out of hand, might even threaten her sisterly image. The next step was to make plans for the taming of her lion, and to direct its power consciously in a positive service. I meet her occasionally, and we both laugh when I inquire into the health of her lion.

THE EXPERIENCE OF THE MALAWIAN CLIENT

As a rule I do not write about what I have not experienced. It therefore seems most presumptuous even to attempt reflection on this topic. After years of working within the culture, as teacher, researcher, now seen as religious formator, I find myself with many others like me who say: "We never really become one with the culture of adoption. There are still responses that surprise us and remain beyond our comprehension. We must constantly resist the temptation to label negative what is simply different. We can too easily stereotype and back off." There is not even scope for research or even simple inquiry because there is no tradition. I can only speculate.

1. Some of the *expectations* of a Malawian client might be:
   • Please understand me. You must walk my roads and meet my family and speak with them in their language.
   • You must know more about life than I do, about my life here and the options before me.
   • Are you aware of the expectations I must live up to, for example, that I am firstborn and what that means?
   • I bring many worlds together within myself. Can you help me sort out who I really am?
   • I fear evil forces that never come near you. I fear witchcraft from a sister living with me in community. How would you face that? Can you help me find freedom and some kind of security?

2. My Malawian client will expect me to *be where* he or she is, in the world I have just been describing, where traditional practices and expectations cross over with modern urban life. If you have never seen an African city, then it will be impossible for you to understand. Clothes, speech, and manners have emerged that bring worlds together but form something entirely new. It is not Western; it is not "village." One must shift back and forth from one world to the other, and God help the inner psyche!

3. "Do I really have to make a choice?"

Grace is a 20-year-old student teacher in a national college of five hundred men and women. She is engaged to a young man of another Christian church. Her parents are staunch Catholics and were distressed by the news. She had never offended, never disobeyed them, and was pulled in two directions. She sought me out when she returned to college from the holidays.

What is going on inside Grace? What does she really want from a counselor? She wants it all—the "it" being all that life offers. She wants her young man, and she wants her parents' blessing on the wedding, and she wants a happy family. She does not really believe that she must make a choice that will eliminate other options. Statistics may prove that women usually follow into the husband's church sooner or later, regardless of whatever promises may be made at the time of marriage. Grace has not explored the consequences of her choice. How much do Mass and the sacraments mean to her, and can she be content with psalms, songs, Bible, and sermons? What of the faith of her children, and their children? Grace did not expect me to ask these kinds of questions. She wanted a simple answer, and there was none. She expected to defend her love, and instead she left me pensive.

4. Where are my deepest loyalties, and *"Can't I be part of two families?"*

One of the more profound questions affecting counseling of women religious is who, precisely, is the individual in relationship to the society. Complete loyalty is maintained where blood family ties are concerned, even while community membership calls for close physical bonding.

The sister before me will have been socialized as a child into the family stream and learned to blend in completely with peers, never rising above others. The sister will have fought for her religious vocation and been misunderstood by the family, which wants new life born into it so as to perpetuate it. Peace is hard won. So now she is a sister, but blood surely runs thicker than water. Sickness, adverse finances, a need for school fees — any family event will come very much to the fore whatever the religious community is living and however binding the vows.

Sisters of Malawi are comfortable with and want a uniform habit; they follow common prayers. Absolute authority seems to have been carried over from traditional models to religious structures. But the sense of belonging to a religious congregation is quite different from that of being one with the family. Blood ties command.

Sr. R. is a Malawian member of an international congregation. Sisters from overseas seem to work hard at getting funding for income-generating projects to "help the poor." But for Sr. R., the poor are *her family*. Why can she not have her garden project to raise funds to send her younger brother and sister to school? *This,* and no other, is her presenting problem. How can the counselor "be with her"?

5. *"Don't lump all the tribes together."*

Genes also affect individual responses in the counseling situation. Tribes vary considerably in their means of survival. There are the more aggressive warrior types; there are those who are more intellectually astute; and finally those who are alive today because of their wits, their ability to confuse the enemy.

My Malawian client might say to me: "Please do not stereotype me. I am unique. There is not one culture for Malawi. Also, you had better be clever, because I can answer your direct question in so many ways! I will be very clever myself to lead you into saying what I want, to sanction what I am aiming at.

"I may speak to you according to how I think *you* expect me to. This is *very* common practice, in fact it is elementary courtesy. I will not confront you, will not defend or argue my point of view, or even try to convince you of what I feel and think.

"I may answer according to the social norms. Regardless of what actually may have happened to me, I will 'make it look right.' I have done this all my life. Truth has many faces.

"I really have the power and control. It will be extremely difficult for me to admit weakness. But deep inside, I am not so sure anymore . . . and sometimes I wonder who I really am. I slip in and out of so many worlds.

"And remember, the taming process may take a bit more time. I am not so sure that I'll ever feel completely free to be fully honest with you. Who is really worthy of trust? But—at some point—we may break through the barriers."

6. *Freedom is as freedom does.*

My Malawian client has a sense of supreme *freedom* that has constantly amazed me. Elders arrange marriages, but the young girl has ways and means to get her man. Foreign powers have moved in and out, occupied the chairs of judges, of business monopoly, of making laws and controlling armies, but the village man or woman stands tall and proud and free. "This is my country. If you have good intentions, you are welcome. Europeans may make wheels turn, but I have my inner secrets that no one can pry from me if I choose to remain silent. Any patronizing attempt to mold me into a preconceived pattern will fall flat. If I feel that you are taking over the direction of our relationship, I will keep my own counsel, smile and agree with you, but I shall depart completely untouched. You might not see me again. On the other hand, I know gratitude, and I never forget when goodness has touched me."

7. *Be Subtle.*

Much more than in counseling within a same culture, my Malawian client will have difficulty communicating the real problem. Family problems over-rule any personal issue and exert strong influence. Jealousies rise up in a thousand forms and hurt unbelievably. "The hardest thing that Christianity ever asked of us is to be able to forgive. We don't." What seemed to be a settled, resolved issue worms its way up again.

Be with me, where I am, even though you cannot imagine how I got there . . . or why I am still there!

PART 4: WHAT HAVE WE BEEN SAYING AND LOOKING AHEAD

PASTORAL COUNSELING AS A PROCESS EXPERIENCED IN AND THROUGH RELATIONSHIP

The process of pastoral counseling unfolds precisely within and through the *relationship* between client and counselor. Let us look more closely at the specific stages, and see how cultural differences may affect them.

Teaming-up. We refer here to how two persons come to the actual counseling relationship. The chemistry between them must be right, the vibrations good. One person has a problem and sees that another has helpful resources. Malawi does not have official mental health centers or counseling services, where anyone may just walk in and "be helped." It is therefore even more sensitive. There will be that certain something between two persons that draws them together. Cultural differences may set up barriers. Any hint of racial, national, or tribal prejudice on either side will eventually have to be dealt with if the counseling ever does pick up. The universal counselor is nonexistent, and *both* counselor and client will have to feel the inner invitation to move into something more personal.

Taming. For the client, a building up of *trust* is crucial. The first encounters will be a "feeling our way" together. The client in any culture must be sufficiently motivated, sufficiently hurting or hungry, and sufficiently able to articulate both the problem and its effect on life. Language becomes extremely important. How listening, receptive, understanding will the counselor appear to be? Discretion and deep respect, with a fidelity to time set apart for encounter, are basic to any culture. All of this is significant for the taming period.

A culturally different concept of *time* will affect the appointments. The mystical hour may need adaptation to today's content. The weekly encounter will be subject to family obligations, unforeseen visitors: "She came in just as I was leaving" implies "therefore I could not leave" and "Why are you surprised that I am late?" Scheduling two persons for a one-hour session each during a four-hour Saturday morning period is, in fact, risky. I seem to hear voices saying that there is such a thing as educating to time-consciousness. Yes, but I better know my people before I try it. *They* will be sensitively appreciative of any effort I make to move into their frame of reference, whether of time or of anything else.

You and Me Becoming Us. How much is the client hurting or wanting? What does the client really want, and have we set a target that we can realistically work toward? The taming will have led to some kind of informal contract. At this point we begin to find the classical transferences, projections, and resistances. Their working out will be the nitty-gritty of the stuff from out of which will hopefully emerge new life.

At this stage theories of counseling come to light. Loyola gave us the space, the freedom, the non-censorship to become the counselors that each had the capacity to be. I can smile at the Howard University supervisor who suggested that Jung and depth psychology were rather heavy for a start, and why didn't I look at Rogers for a beginning! For the rest, it was encouragement to pursue what intuition and classroom exposure might inspire ... under supervision.

Because we are all humans together, I do believe that theories evolved in one culture have some chance of being applicable in another, provided there is a sensitive awareness of differences throughout. Rogerian empathy, Gestalt directness, behavioristic immediacy, depth imagery . . . why not?

It is the journeying together that does it, of that I am increasingly certain. It can be physical attending, psychological support or sharing of insight, moving maybe into prayer and communion. As differences, clashes, and upsets occur within the relationship, they are dealt with and bonds of unity are forged. *That* is what gives hope for new living. Probably my most rewarding moments in ministry are when we face a problem together in prayer. The prayer must come *after* all is said and done. It comes when we know our helplessness to control events and to fashion others "according to our image and likeness." We let go and let God be God, with the power emerging precisely as we *agree* before our Maker.

I cherish the episode with Mrs. R.

We had contracted for spiritual accompaniment. The encounters centered around her human journey with all its ups and downs, whatever was her major concern at that moment. From there we would look at how this affected her walk with God.

She had mothered eight children, all living. Her husband had abandoned her during her last pregnancy, and she had turned inward to her faith for comfort and strength.

She came one day with the problem that one of her sons was becoming a thief. He had finished high school and obtained a reasonable job, but the salary could not support the kind of lifestyle he wanted. The latest incident had been at the home of relatives, where he had made off with expensive work tools. The wife was toying with calling in the police. Mrs. R. had horrible visions of what happens to thieves—beatings and so on. She had checked out the cost of what had been stolen and was shocked. How to make amends?

We talked it over. She knew that at a certain point her children were no longer her own, and that she could no longer make decisions for them. She left me that day with the prayer project of experiencing with greater awareness the great love and concern God has for each of his children. We did not pray together on this occasion, as sometimes happens, but after her departure I went into our tiny chapel and sat in silence. I held her out to the Lord, wordlessly visualizing her in God's Love. I became an intercessory presence. After a certain time, I knew it was enough. For a couple of days, she returned off and on to my conscious awareness and the mental gesture was repeated.

At our next meeting she reported that for two days after seeing me she was obsessed with worries and images worse than before. Each time they came she would fight them off and try to surrender her son to God. Then, on the morning of the third day (resurrection?), as she was waking up, she heard an inner voice tell her quite distinctly:

"Ndine Mwini Nzeru." Translated, this comes to something like, "I am the Lord of all knowing." Her immediate reaction was to question where that voice had come from (note the natural discernment of spirits). She was then flooded with the deepest of consolations. God knew all, had all the means in hand, knew what was going to be done. Her burden lifted. If conscious memory tempted to bring back the dread, she had only to recall the words interiorly and feel peace again. The struggle was finished.

I cannot know that my prayer had any bearing on the case. I only know that there are some clients with whom I must pray, others whom I pray for, and still others that I seem to forget, even though I had intended to remember them.

I am truly convinced that the work we go though during the counseling hour—searching, putting into words, uncovering and unmasking—makes the human bonding ripe for the leap of faith. I went into pastoral counseling because I had felt that in healing prayer we might easily pray away symptoms, which soon returned because roots had not been touched. Counseling is that journey into the interior whereby we bring to light what is in the depths. We do this as best we can, with whatever honest means we have. Then, "the power of God at work in us can do infinitely more than we dare ask or even dream" (Ephesians 3:20). It is a beautiful part of my pastoral counseling ministry. We have by now far transcended the cultural barriers. In fact, they seem to recede into irrelevancy.

Toward Termination. "It is the time you have wasted for your rose that makes your rose so important. . . . You become responsible forever for what you have tamed" (*The Little Prince,* Antoine de Saint-Exupery, p. 71). Encounters will be spaced out, no longer scheduled, but the relationship lives on. People who feel they have been helped by me seem to "light up" when we meet. No words are needed. Often, a follow-up workshop will be the occasion to pick up where we left off, provide another brief encounter, then get on with the living. Taming is indeed forever.

Toward a Theory of Counseling

I sit back and with my mind's eye review the decade. Youth counseling flowing from a religious education class encounter . . . I had only to walk in and set up the stage. Formation and ongoing formation programs for women and men religious leading into the privileged one-on-one encounter. . . . That had to be an invitation and has only gradually called me forth. I wondered if I could even call it counseling. I often envied my peers who were working under supervision and could discuss cases with colleagues. My setting had been so completely different. Yet, I am changed. I feel that life is left in suspense if I simply "proclaim good news" without the interpersonal encounter.

What wants to grow now is the far more personal and comprehensive aspect of *spiritual accompaniment*. This has been offered and is being accepted by those who have least access to anything of the sort, namely the laity. My own at-homeness with the Ignatian *Exercises,* stemming from a religious lifetime of apostolic spirituality, has recently been capped off by the Guelph Ontario Institute. The search for God in daily life embodies the whole person, while pastoral counseling remains at the core of it.

I am incapable of formulating any new theory of pastoral counseling, because I am still unwrapping the Loyola gift of ten years ago. It still feels fresh and poses new challenges as I myself undergo changes and am helped on the way.

THE FUTURE OF PASTORAL COUNSELING

I am no prophet, but I do see needs and possibilities. The AIDS crisis is definitely putting counseling on the Malawian map. I see pastoral counseling as being full of potential for health, healing, fuller life. The need is first for trained counselors, who could form a church or interfaith team. There is a definite increasing interest in the field. In the past few months I have met several Malawian sisters who have had studies in spirituality, religious formation, with exposure to pastoral counseling. They are keen on learning more about it. One or the other would surely qualify for the Loyola program, and I could wish them nothing better. Finances remain a limiting factor.

Let us however start with what is. In four months, a one week first-ever workshop on pastoral counseling will be sponsored by the Association of Religious at the national level. Some thirty to forty sisters are expected. I have carte blanche to conduct it as I see fit. My planner is very much at work!

First, someone to work with: I have been able to coopt one of the sisters mentioned above. She is keenly perceptive, aware of her own cultural stance, and just back from studies preparing for retreat work and spiritual direction.

Second, content: One day to look at the human person, another to look at growth, followed by two days on counseling skills. We keep the last day for specialized counseling, for example, AIDS. I will bring a Jungian understanding of the psyche, talk of developmental stages as we see them exploring growth patterns. My Malawian counterpart will reflect on and present the "African" understanding of the person and growth. Group work will be used to personalize this.

How to initiate basic counseling skills is the question. Could I tempt any of my Loyola mentors to take a holiday in the tropics and be our guest? It is a delightful dream, to say the least.

We want to make it as simple and practical as possible. The very first night of arrival, they will be paired off according to already existing trusting relationships. Each day will have a privileged hour, where they attempt to taste what counseling can be—both as client and as counselor. Third and fourth days will lead us through listening, empathic responses, physical attending, body language, and non-verbal communication . . . according to how the Spirit moves us. We are tempted to try some psychodrama, Gestalt activities, and so on.

There will be little future for pastoral counseling unless there are reinforcements. Persons with training and skills will have to be present, make themselves known, then sell their product much as we have done in our countries. There is still a long way to go, and Malawians will most effectively do it themselves. I believe that Loyola gave us the best, and is in fact already serving people of all "tribes, tongues, and nations."

5

ZAMBIA

EILEEN KEANE

Sister Eileen Keane, missionary doctor working in various hospital situations in Africa for over thirty years, describes how her more recent training in pastoral counseling has assisted her medical ministry with the Batonga of Zambia. Returning to Zambia in 1989 to find that the majority of hospital patients were young people between the ages of 15 and 45 who test positive for HIV, Sister Eileen called upon her pastoral counseling training to train volunteer nurses, men and women, who have the intimate knowledge of the culture and the language skills to deal with the nuances of multiple dialects, as pastoral care workers. Dr. Keane draws on her personal faith in the mystery of redemption as she assists persons with AIDS in discovering hope and a renewed ability to live with dignity and meaning.

I had been working with the Batonga for six years prior to going to Loyola in 1987. During those years I became acquainted with their culture and acquired a rather skimpy knowledge of their language—Citonga. Since my return, the learning process has continued and been stimulated by my tentative steps into the world of pastoral counseling.

To the stereotypical work-oriented European or white person, the Batonga are happy, relaxed, and people-oriented. Greetings and enquiries about themselves and their families are far more important than getting a job done. I have always been struck by the Tonga person's positive self-image. This must surely come from earliest experiences—for the first two years of life a Tonga child is in constant contact with its mother, being carried on her back or suckled at her breast. The mother constitutes the child's entire world and the child grows and develops surrounded by a sense of security. Upon weaning, this secure world may suddenly disappear and the child may be given to a grandparent or uncle and aunt to be reared. Very soon such a child is expected to work in this other family and, if lucky, may be sent to school eventually with his or her "brothers" and "sisters." A person's "father" or "mother" or "brother" or "sister" may refer to the people or family members with whom he or she has lived. An uncle or aunt frequently acts as mother or father to the child of any member of the clan or family. This leads to complicated situations within the extended family.

Rituals exist for all major events in a Tonga person's life—birth, naming, initiation into adulthood, marriage, parenthood, death. The omission or ignoring of any of these is likely to cause disharmony in the family. Long before Western medicine became available, sickness and disease were the concern of the diviners and witch doctors or traditional healers. The diviners were particularly powerful because they were able to point to the person who *caused* the illness in any patients brought to them. The concept of an infection caused by a bacterium or a virus is still very difficult to accept. Very often when the person named as having caused an illness pays whatever fine or penalty is recommended by the diviner, it is found that the patient improves or gets better completely. Similarly, when a person is diagnosed as suffering from "spirits," what looks to the Western observer like an attack of hysteria, the diviner or traditional healer can treat this swiftly and effectively. An illness is a problem for all of the family, not for the sick individual. Significant relatives must be consulted before deciding on a course of action, that is, whether to seek out one or other traditional healer or diviner or to go to a hospital. Any person coming to the hospital has tried traditional healing or medicine before coming.

The world of ancestral spirits is a very real one for the Batonga. It is important to respect them, to honor good spirits and avoid evil ones. Similarly there is a strong belief in witchcraft and the power of diviners and witch doctors. Whenever anything adverse happens to a person, family, or community, these traditional experts are consulted. It is not surprising, then, that the one overriding emotion observable among the Batonga is *fear*. This leads to mistrust, particularly of strangers. This fear is the reason for having family discussions prior to making any decisions about the course of action to be followed in the case of illness, disease, death, and funeral ceremonies. People are seen to go on several days' journey to attend a funeral and bring some gift to the bereaved family; if this is not done they may be suspected of having caused the dead person's illness and even death. A spouse who does not grieve and cry for a dead partner may be suspected, hence the ritualized *Kulila* at a hospital mortuary or in the home. Individual privacy is totally submerged by family and community involvement and responsibility for the individual.

I have described only the aspects of Tonga culture that mainly concern health and disease; it would take several volumes to describe all customs,

beliefs, and practices. Anthropologist Elizabeth Colson has written extensively on these. I focused on health and disease, though very superficially
indeed, because of my own orientation and profession as a medical doctor.

It is basically very important for any person wishing to engage in health
care among the Batonga to understand and accept the people's attitude to
health and disease. Their actions are governed by the social imperatives I
have discussed. So often I have explained a patient's illness and condition
to the family and been assured by them that all is understood, only to learn
later that the family held its own meeting at home and consulted one or
several diviners to find out who caused the illness. The diviner is paid a
fee, and the culprit is forced to pay, too. Paradoxically, I, who may have
adequately and successfully treated the patient's pneumonia or other infection, am not paid at all by the family!

Not surprisingly, as a missionary doctor working in various hospital situations in Africa over the past thirty years, I have often pondered on the
mystery of suffering and sought some theological approach to it. The agony
of our Lord in Gethsemene before his passion and death has given me
considerable insight. Jesus entered the garden with his friends, knowing
Judas had gone off to betray him and that he would soon be captured. The
awful reality of his situation was borne in on him and, being fully human,
he became terrified, did not want it, could not face it. This was the essence
of his struggle, his agony; that is, the tension between his will and the
Father's—"Not my will but thine be done" (Luke 22:43). He had to say
that, because in all truth his will was very much to escape and avoid the
suffering ahead. He remained a long time there and at some point his will
and the Father's became *one*. With this fusion of wills came a most remark-
able transformation in Jesus. He returned to the disciples with a spring in
his step and newfound authority and strength in his voice and whole bearing: "Rise, let us go! My betrayer is close at hand already" (Mark 14:42).
Judas and the priests and soldiers arrived, and Jesus asks, "Whom do you
seek?" They say, "Jesus of Nazareth." He answers, "I am he." The authority and assurance in his reply causes them to fall backward (John 18:6).
Jesus leaves the garden a completely different man from the fearful one
who entered it. The transformation occurred when he ceased to struggle
and gradually but fully accepted the reality of his situation and said an
unconditional yes to it. There is a world of a difference here between
surrendering or resigning himself to it and actually accepting it totally. Over
the years I have witnessed similar transformations in some patients and
have, indeed, experienced something of it in my own life when I had to
undergo cardiac surgery and had my own struggle with the Father's will.

Jesus is not only the model of a person in need of healing, but he is also
the physician, the counselor par excellence. This is shown very powerfully
in his meeting with the man sitting at the pool of Bethsaida. Jesus' question
is addressed to all who suffer in mind, heart, or body: "Do you want to be
well again?" (John 5:7). No amount of medicine, no surgery, is of any avail

unless the sick or wounded person really wishes to be whole, to be healed. Kahlil Gibran writes:

> Your pain is the breaking of the shell that encloses your understanding.
>
> Even as the stone of the fruit must break, that its heart may stand in the sun, so must you know pain. . . .
>
> Much of your pain is self-chosen. It is the bitter potion by which the physician within you heals your sick self (Gibran 1946, 60-61).

I have dwelt on this subject of suffering and dealt with the concepts of health and disease within the framework of Tonga culture because it is within this context I have striven to introduce pastoral counseling. For me, pastoral counseling is a ministry within the healing ministry. I have no difficulty in recognizing myself as a wounded healer and identifying with Henri Nouwen's words:

> For the minister is called to recognize the sufferings of his time in his own heart and make that recognition the starting point of his service. Whether he tries to enter into a dislocated world, relate to a convulsive generation, or speak to a dying man, his service will not be perceived as authentic unless it comes from a heart wounded by the suffering about which he speaks (Nouwen 1972, xvi).

And again:

> Making one's own wounds a source of healing, therefore, does not call for a sharing of superficial personal pains but for a constant willingness to see one's own pain and suffering as rising from the depth of the human condition which all men share (Nouwen 1972, 88).

Pastoral counseling within the healing ministry is becoming absolutely essential in Zambia today because of the reality of HIV infection. A growing and alarming number of patients are affected and are confronted with the reality of an illness for which neither Western nor traditional medicine has a cure. Before the AIDS era, and certainly over the latter half of the twentieth century, Western-trained health professionals could confidently offer hope of a cure for most illnesses. Now we know that once a person is infected there is nothing we can yet do to the virus—only wait in hope! Traditional healers are similarly powerless. Fear, suspicion, mistrust, angry denial, blaming, guilt, and hurt all are showing their ugly faces in our daily contacts.

On my return from Loyola in early 1989 the situation already described had become well established. The medical wards witnessed to a sense of puzzlement and disarray among the staff. Young people between the ages of 15 and 45 constituted the majority of the medical patients, and many of those tested positive for HIV. There were too many for any one person to deal with in a counseling situation. I struggled also to define for myself my own role. I am a medical doctor and am seen to be one by my patients, even when and if I approach them as "clients." They look to me for a cure, an answer, a solution to their problem. I realize how limited my ability to speak Citonga is, and also how I am seen to be a European and therefore not part of the Batonga culture. I understood these limitations very clearly prior to my introduction to pastoral counseling.

Also, among the rural population, the age, sex, and race or tribe of a counselor is a very significant factor; an elderly man is most likely to be helped by an older male of the same tribe and so forth. The skills I learned at Loyola had to be passed on, communicated, to Zambian women and men who would, in turn, become counselors. I invited nurses, male and female, to come for classes, and so began weekly meetings during which I shared my understanding of a helping relationship and introduced the small group to the basics of counseling. It was inspiring to observe the reactions of the group to the ideas first advocated by Carl Rogers, "that individuals have within themselves vast resources for self understanding and for altering self concepts, basic attitudes and self-directed behavior" (Rogers 1980). The qualities of genuineness or congruence, acceptance or caring, "unconditional positive regard" and empathic understanding, were readily seen as necessary in dealing with people infected with HIV presented to us in the hospital.

Some months after our classes commenced a government initiative was undertaken to train counselors. Six of our group went to the Provincial Center for a week's introductory course. They met participants from all over the province. On their return they appeared much more enthusiastic about their new roles. Evidently what I had been teaching them had been confirmed and they had a head-start on the other participants! A month's practical work followed and then a second week for evaluation. Through these introductory experiences they came to do pretest and post-test counseling. One or two nurses were assigned a ward and given the opportunity to do this initial counseling. Many found themselves in situations of crisis intervention before many days passed.

Our weekly meetings became case conferences or small-group supervisory sessions. I personally learned as much as the nurses. Here they were, within their own culture, translating the concepts of pastoral counseling into their way of understanding them. It was surprising to note their surprise at the reactions, particularly of denial, in their clients and their difficulty in establishing a relationship of trust. For many of our clients, HIV stands as a dreadful enemy which stigmatizes. Since 99 percent of cases occur through heterosexual transmission, and since sexually transmitted diseases have been well known and widespread prior to the late 1970s, one realizes that the stigma stems from the fact that there is no cure for HIV. AIDS is known to be fatal. Death is an imminent possibility. This is the real difficulty. Nobody likes to face death. For our clients two reactions prevail: denial and insistence on confidentiality on the part of the client, and stigmatization on the part of the community. The first young man who declared his HIV-positive status on the national television was shunned by his neighbors. As he rode to work no one would sit beside him, and the conductor demanded that he pay for the empty seat also!

Stigmatization is more understandable in Tonga culture than the issue of confidentiality. In a culture where all major issues are dealt with in the context of community or family, the cry for confidentiality regarding HIV infection begets alienation and isolation, a very uncomfortable, new feeling for many. The need for confidentiality arises from fear. As one client said to me, "I do not want to tell my wife, she must never know. Her family would make big trouble for me!" He died without telling her. The fear in many instances is not unfounded. Another man told me that the family of his wife, who had died of AIDS two weeks previously, had told him they were taking him to court for giving her the disease.

Many problems have surfaced in our meetings, and those presented are new experiences to these student counselors. One student had a young mother of a child with AIDS and discussed the implications of this. The mother agreed to being tested, and it was suggested that she bring her husband for an interview. She calmly agreed. Two days later the husband came in a very agitated state asking for the nurse. When he found her, he said, "My wife told me that I have AIDS and should make my will immediately." This quantum leap from what the woman was told to what she conveyed to her husband was not unique. Many instances of such exaggeration exist. They constantly challenge the student to maintain a relationship of trust with the client, even when that trust is not honored. I personally counseled a man who was HIV positive and had pulmonary tuberculosis. "John" was a public official, a civil servant holding official authority in an area called a ward. In a few initial sessions we simply covered the reality of his situation. I sensed his fear of death and fatalism: "Why bother treating TB when you can't treat HIV?" I suggested that there were grounds for hope, other ways of thinking which would influence how he was feeling. He seemed to agree, but some days later he came to me in distress. He informed me that a visitor to the ward had read his hospital notes and told his wife about his diagnosis. She had run away with her child. He needed to go home immediately. We let him go and of course took steps to ensure that notes were not read by non-medical staff in the future. I felt guilty at being the indirect cause of this family upheaval. Some weeks later our TB clinical officer came to me smiling. "You remember John?" he said. "That story he told you was all lies! He just wanted to go and get African medicine! His wife did not run away for the reason he said. She had gone to a funeral." Yet again I wondered, "When will I ever really understand? Really be able to trust?" I met John six months later in his village. He freely acknowledged that he had gone to another town to a traditional healer and received two kinds of medicine. He felt one of these medicines helped a little, but now he wanted to come back for Western medicine. Despite this, his attendance for treatment was irregular and his trust in a good outcome was poor. He died at home. The time from diagnosis of illness and initial interview to his death was relatively short. He was unable to grasp at hope.

Christeta, a nurse on our staff, has a different history. She came to me for a medical checkup shortly after I returned from Loyola. The notes she brought with her were not very detailed, and I was unsure of her HIV status. Clinically I suspected she was positive. She volunteered this information herself. At the conclusion of our meeting she remarked, "I would be better off dead!" Addressing this needed more time than was available in a medical clinic, so we made an appointment for that evening. She calmly explained her very difficult home situation, her clear knowledge of her precarious health, and her overriding concern for her two children after her death. "Surely," I thought, "there must be some ray of hope." I asked about her concept of God and whether she liked scripture, as so many Zambians do. She replied that she had two bibles at home — one in English and one in Citonga — and she read some passage daily. We met again. Then she became ill and had to be admitted. I visited her in hospital on a number of occasions. One day I suggested she read Isaiah 43:1-6 and substitute her name for Jacob and Israel:

> But now thus says Yahweh
> Who created you, Christeta
> Who formed you, Christeta;
> Do not be afraid, for I have redeemed you.

As she read on, she sat more erectly and her voice became stronger. Then she suddenly stopped and said, "Ah doctor, there is no need to say anything more!" I left her. She was duly discharged and went on sick leave. About four months later she returned saying she was well enough to work. She was given a lighter job. We did not have regular sessions, but whenever I met her and asked how she was she looked at me with an air of confidence and said, "I'm OK." Soon she was down with another infection and came through that saying, "I'm getting better." Then a drug reaction occurred and she made little of that. She had a purpose in life and a sure hope in Yahweh.

As time goes on I have become more and more aware of the impact of AIDS upon women. Others have had this awareness long before me. African women have established their own international group: Society for

Women and AIDS in Africa (SWAA). At our group meetings I asked the nurses/counselors if they would like to form a branch. They took up the idea enthusiastically and called a meeting. More than a hundred women came. I insisted that the nurses facilitate and organize the meeting; I would make a few preliminary remarks. I simply pointed out all the functions these women were fulfilling, and being taken for granted in doing so — plowing the fields with the oxen, carrying firewood and water, bearing and caring for children, cooking for the family, caring for sick relatives in the hospital, and so on. All the women present agreed with what was said. Many knew that their husbands were promiscuous yet expected them to ignore this, even to the extent of ignoring the possibility of their becoming infected with HIV.

One practice, which to twentieth-century Western minds is hard to accept, is that widows are expected to become the wives of their deceased husband's brother, or at least be "cleansed" by the brother having sexual intercourse with the widow. This is known as ritual cleansing; the widow is thereby cleansed and released from the spirit of her dead husband. The implications of this practice for HIV transmission are obvious! Should the widow refuse, her husband's family takes away from her, literally, all her worldly possessions. These possessions, and she herself, are considered the family's property.

At that first meeting I noticed a young mother breastfeeding her baby in the front seat. I asked the gathering, "Suppose this woman's husband dies and suppose all of you came to support this young woman. Do you think the husband's family could take all her belongings away?" A resounding no was the reply. They divided into small groups and discussed the various aspects of their lives on which AIDS impinged. The most common topic from all groups and the one chosen for the next meeting was, "How to Say No to our Husbands!" This may seem strange to Western feminists!

A few weeks after my return from Loyola I spoke to all the health staff within the District of Monze on the medical facts about AIDS to ensure that our health education program was clearly understood by all. During the "coffee break" I noticed two nurses, mature married women, walking outside together and looking obviously disturbed. I joined them and asked what their problem was. Together they replied, "Doctor, we are afraid to become pregnant!" For thirty seconds I was lost, then it dawned on me. Each woman knew that her husband had several ongoing liaisons and also realized that the likelihood of becoming HIV infected was great. And they knew pregnancy and HIV was not a very healthy state. Yet there was no way either could even indicate her suspicions to her husband!

Another nurse was in my office one day and said, "You know, doctor, we women, we are 'in problem' " (a lovely idiomatic expression). "Before this AIDS we could do our work, go home, look after our children, and even earn enough to send them to school. Now with AIDS, we know how our husbands are, how they behave, so one day they will bring home this virus to us and then what will happen to our children?" Maybe SWAA will, in time, provide a solution. It is a most suitable forum for group counseling.

I have dwelt at length on the issue of AIDS in the context of the healing ministry because that is the reality in which I find myself, and it is the context in which I have done pastoral counseling. Because of my medical background and the numbers of patients, I have not been able to practice, personally, to any great extent, as a pastoral counselor. As stated, my difficulty with the local language precludes working with clients who do not speak English. l have therefore been limited to helping a small number of English-speaking clients. Even in these situations I am seen by the client as doctor, and the person reacts to me as a patient, that is expecting a cure, a solution. My major role to date has been in training Zambian staff and journeying with them in a supervisory capacity. The nurses/counselors act initially as caring, educating, health workers with the patients who come to them and with the patients' family members. Since the early months of 1989 we have established a Community Home Based Care (CHBC) Team for patients with AIDS (PWA). Patients from within the District of Monze on discharge are taken home, and the family is drawn into caring for the person. Monthly visits by the team to the person's home continue this process. The care and fidelity of the CHBC Team builds up a trusting relationship with the PWA and his or her family.

I have given a few instances of my experiences with clients. Our nurse counselors have shared theirs. We have all become aware of the tension between the individual and the community, which is a new phenomenon with the advent of AIDS. Formerly a person shared in the family and sought support in any problem. Now, very often, the person isolates himself or herself and is unable to function very well in this strange environment. The counselor is sometimes made a scapegoat by the client and caught between the client and the family. The level of social stigmatization is such that a spouse will resist informing the partner regarding HIV positive status while apparently wishing to do so. Even when the partner is informed, he or she is so overwhelmed by denial that he or she will come with the spouse and say, "He (She) did not tell me anything." Outside the context of AIDS and counseling, this is a characteristic tactic of relatives wishing to gain all information directly from the health worker.

I feel that all of us who are trying to do some counseling experience resistance and difficulty in establishing and maintaining a trusting relationship with clients. Frequently we have felt a client to be calm and fully aware of the situation, but subsequent behavior and interaction with family members demonstrates the opposite. There have, of course, been exceptions. We have instances of persons coming to a state of saying "I have never been so happy in all my life" just days or hours before they died.

Clients experience counseling as a new approach, especially within a hospital setting. They come to a doctor or nurse expecting a diagnosis and treatment leading to cure. The suggestion that they have the only answer within themselves demands a major turn around. Clients strive to look *outside* for help to take away the problem. This behavior may lead to very rash activity, such as selling all material possessions and making a will ("I'm going to die very soon, I have AIDS!"), or to complete denial ("There is nothing wrong with me. The counselor told me I am OK" or "Nobody ever told me I had the HIV.") There is also denial about the kind of lifestyle the client has lived. Behavior change, once a sexually active life has commenced, takes place very, very slowly if at all. "This cannot happen to me" is the typical response to a warning about the danger of developing HIV infection. Even with educated clients the cultural social imperatives have a more powerful influence than rational healthy behavior.

An example of this is in the case of a young woman, a teacher. She had two children and was ill during her second pregnancy. At that time she was found to be HIV positive. Her second child subsequently died. It was pointed out to her that she should avoid future pregnancies. She appeared to agree with this. A year later she was admitted with a miscarriage and again counseled regarding further pregnancies. A year later she returned and, filled with joy, announced, "I think I am pregnant." This behavior results from the social expectation that the woman should bear children. Women in this culture readily choose to take the risk of pregnancy and even of bearing a child who may die after two or three years rather than to live in good health and remain childless. They know that at death the body of an infertile woman is not respected. This final disgrace must be avoided at all costs.

From all the foregoing it must be clear that the relationship between the pastoral counselor and the client is fraught with difficulties and misconceptions. Clients tend to be dependent, and the pastoral counselor, coming already from a health care background, struggles to change this. A caring, empathic, non-judgmental attitude on the part of the pastoral counselor certainly has a profoundly positive effect on the relationship. Clients have commented on this as a new experience. Nurses who go out in the CHBC Team decided not to wear uniforms. This is another step in breaking a stereotypical barrier. Respect for a client as a person begets almost inordinate self-confidence, born of the positive self-image most Tonga people have. When a trusting relationship is finally established, the client often invites the counselor to come and speak with the family. This is a vital step in the relationship because of the cultural importance of the family and community. The client needs to deal with whatever issue arises within the family; inviting the pastoral counselor into this milieu is a mark of progress in the relationship.

The process of counseling in our context may not appear similar to that in a Western milieu. However, the different counseling theories can be utilized depending on the personal preference of the pastoral counselor. Because the majority of clients either have AIDS or are relatives of persons with AIDS, pastoral counseling may take the form of crisis intervention. If this is successful the process ends there, at least for some time. Clients need to deal with issues within the family setting. Leaving space for this to take place is important. At a home visit often a relative will express a client's concern, not the client personally. Concerns are also often expressed indirectly, perhaps by narrating a story about some absent person. The alert pastoral counselor will understand what is going on and enter into it. Thus the client does not lose face while dealing with the issue in question.

It is clear that we are very much at the beginning stages of pastoral counseling here. The various theories and approaches practiced in the West can and need to be adapted to our situation. I have already referred to the central Rogerian hypothesis that each person has adequate resources for altering attitudes and behavior. I am convinced our clients are no different in this respect from people in any other part of the world. Our clients' behavior arises from the ways of thinking and believing practiced within the Tonga culture. The cognitive approach, in an effort to change faulty beliefs and practices, appears to me to be valuable. I believe it is possible for our clients to reindoctrinate themselves with different beliefs and values, even though cultural beliefs and values are very strong. Even in the face of AIDS, I believe it is possible for mature individuals to accept themselves fully, to live with the uncertainty of the future, and to continue to have an effective interest in society. This approach can also be applied to family and group situations. It has been used effectively among groups of community leaders—only among such as these can beliefs about the power and activity of ancestral spirits be altered. The practice of ritual cleansing referred to has been modified in three out of five chiefdoms using an application of this approach. Community counseling as opposed to individual counseling appears to me to have greater potential among the Batonga because of their very close-knit communal way of living. Additionally, only in the community setting can a behaviorist approach be effective; only as a community can debilitating behaviors dictated by cultural beliefs be altered. The community can focus on action, what behavior needs to be changed, and decide how to change it. The community can be enabled to take communal responsibility for practices and alter factors that affect faulty behavior. Even though cultural practices continue as a result of historical determinants and are, therefore, very difficult to change, one current behavior—increasing promiscuity resulting from rapid urbanization—can be altered by the community setting definite goals. Similarly, peer-group counseling can be utilized to deal with peer-group pressures in schools. The young man who publicly declared his HIV-positive status practiced outreach counseling in the Lusaka schools, in this context.

Underpinning all counseling activity is the awareness of the presence of God, *Leza Taata*, in everyone's life. There are at least ten different Christian sects, some of them quite fundamentalist, in Monze town. Every client has some Christian affiliation, the major group being Seventh Day Adventist, which is fundamentally scripture oriented. The Bible, the Word of God, is held sacred by all. Christeta, reading Isaiah 43, is only one of very many clients who have discovered hope and a reason to live in the Word of God. Patients in the wards have been seen sharing scripture passages with others less well than themselves and together coming to a fuller way of living. One European visitor who observed this remarked, "I would not have believed this unless I had seen it myself!" We have truly observed that for our patients

> faith becomes an opportunity to listen to God, hope an invitation to see God in different ways, love an example of true service of God and prayer a chance to experience God as never before (Wicks 1988).

AIDS is looked upon in all its dire negative aspects. It must be acknowledged that never before have we seen so many people come to a state of deep happiness and joy—yes, confidence too—in the face of death. Through pastoral care of the terminally ill many become signs of hope for others and in their own unique, though perhaps small ways, resemble Jesus walking out of Gethsemene.

What future do I see for pastoral counseling? I have no hesitation in believing that for as long as AIDS is with us here, pastoral counseling will be a major force in dealing with it. Through work with those with AIDS the value of pastoral counseling will be appreciated and most likely will be sought in other areas of people's lives. There is a pressing need for adequately trained pastoral counselors in Zambia today. The training provided to date equips counselors only for crisis intervention or short-term counseling situations. The dangers of embarking on counseling without adequate skills are only too obvious. It is imperative, therefore, that more suitable and longer training courses be provided, preferably within the country. It is also necessary that those who undergo training are adequately supervised and supported as they commence their ministry. I have mentioned my own difficulty with the language. There are several Bantu dialects in this country. Persons choosing to practice pastoral counseling should have an intimate knowledge of these. This is a basic requisite, just as basic as having a suitable personality and counseling skills. Many Zambians can converse with ease in at least four dialects so, for them, language is not a problem. Zambians, like all of us, are products of their own culture and thus possess an understanding of their clients' frame of reference that is acquired slowly and incompletely by outsiders, if at all. Certainly the theories, practices, and approaches to counseling already recognized in the West are excellent stepping stones to counseling in Africa. It is my conviction, however, and indeed my hope, that Africans, from whatever tribe or culture, will take these stepping stones and fashion them into bricks with which to build their own counseling edifice. This edifice may appear to outsiders to be a mud hut, but if it provides the right climate and environment and suitably adapted skills, it will serve Zambians better than the skyscrapers and grand colleges of the West.

6

GHANA

JOSEPH GHUNNEY

Reverend Joseph K. Ghunney, descendent of the Akan people of Ghana, West Africa, offers rare insight into the world view of his culture as he reflects on the delicate task of integrating Western theories of counseling within the context of African culture.

An understanding of the Akan requires insight into the relationship of the individual to one's family, clan and tribe. It is difficult for a Westerner to understand the impact of the "extended family." Knowledge of the symbolic language and myths that permeate the Akan culture is also essential to an understanding of the Akan experience. Pastoral counseling in Ghana, as in other African countries, needs to be integrated within the context of the multi-faceted world view of each African culture.

Traditionally, the African has a way of resolving life problems quite different from counseling in the western world. Pastoral counseling as practiced in the West is a new discipline in Africa.

After completing the Masters Program in Pastoral Counseling at Loyola College in Maryland, where I learned many theories in counseling, I returned home to Ghana in West Africa with the hope of practicing the theories I had learned in the West. I realized, however, that though the theories I learned were good ones, most of them were not practicable in Ghana. The only way I could succeed in the counseling situations there was to contextualize and graft what I had learned with the Ghanian culture.

For example, I like person-centered therapy, a nondirective approach developed by Carl Rogers based on a subjective view of human experience. It gives more responsibility to the client in dealing with problems (Corey

1982). But unfortunately, the African client has a world view that makes it impossible for him or her to take responsibility *alone* in solving problems. This world view will be discussed in this chapter, in which I attempt to record my own evolving theory in the practice of pastoral counseling in Africa. Let me underline the need to take the African culture into serious consideration as I use the Western framework in speaking of counseling in Africa.

Boia (1973) defines culture as:

> The accumulation of the group's experience; it is the way of solving the problems of life's demands and needs; and the attitudes, folkways, mores, ways of behaving, and feelings that have been invented, tested, approved and perpetuated in a particular peoples' history. All these habits, ways of doing things are institutions for meeting economic needs, organizing political relations, expressing religious worship, and regulating marriage and family relations (p. 137).

Africa is a large continent with many different cultures. One could travel just twenty miles away from one village to another and find that the two villages have different cultures. It is, therefore, impossible to address all the cultures in Africa. As the basis for this chapter, I will use the culture with which I am most familiar, that of the Akans.

The Akan people are composed of two groups: the Fanti speaking and the Twi speaking. They trace their descent matrilineally. They have a common language, but with some degree of dialectical differences. They also have common cultural patterns in their socio-political institutions. For the Akan, there is no dichotomy between the physical world and the spiritual world, the sacred and the secular, the mundane and the holy. Religion is all-pervasive in the Akans' ontology (Williamson 1974; Pobee 1979; Lartey 1987).

THE AKAN'S WORLD VIEW

The everyday life of the Akan is permeated with religion. Akans believe that this universe was created by a Supreme Being, who is associated with the sky. According to Akan mythology, he used to live very close to the world of humans. The sky, which is his abode, was so close to humans that they could touch it. There was an old woman who used a long pestle to pound her *fufu*, an Akan dish, and her pestle always hit the sky. Despite continuous warnings from the Supreme Being, she continued her pounding and the Supreme Being retreated upward out of her reach. Even though he has retreated upward, he continues to have relations with humans. To the Akan, knowledge of the Supreme Being is innate. His relationship with humans is expressed through myths, legends, and proverbs. The Akan proverb, *"Obi nkyere abofra Onyame,"* literally translates as: "Nobody teaches the child who God is." This is indicative of the Akans' innate belief in the Supreme Being. Most of the appellations for the Supreme Being describe how humans experience him rather than abstract knowledge of him.

The Supreme Being is *Obaatan* — parent — and his parenthood is described in the phrase: *"Obaatan, Onyame nyim awo,"* meaning, "The Supreme Being, unlike other parents, knows how to care for his children." Even though male anthropomorphic language is used to describe him, his activities are not limited to a male role. As *Obaatan*, he functions as both male and female.

Most people respond to greetings by referring to what the Supreme Being has done for them. For example, "How are you?" is typically answered, "By God's grace. . . . " The Supreme Being is also seen as the helper of the helpless and the vindicator of the innocent. A person who feels unfairly treated would summon the oppressor with the words, "I give all to God" or "God would pay you back." An Akan proverb "It is God who scratches the body of an animal without a tail showing how he cares for the needy."

When the Supreme Being decided to go upward because of the diso-bedience of the old woman, he decided to delegate some of his powers to lesser deities. Until the dawn of Christianity, and even now, many people believe that the lesser deities are God's children, *Onyame Mba*. These lesser deities are called *Abosom*. The *Abosom* animate rivers, lagoons, seas, rocks, trees, hills, mountains, stones, and so forth. They can make their abode in anything on earth. Many Western writers of African traditional religion wrongly posit that Africans worship these objects, but it is the deity that is worshiped; whatever it resides in is only revered and respected as a holy place.

There are individual, family, community, and tribal deities. For example, since my paternal home worships *Alcrama*, every descendant from that paternal root sees *Alcrama* as his or her God. However, *Penkye Otu* is the god of my maternal family and the god of all people from the *Effutus* tribe. Unlike the Supreme Being, these lesser gods have powers limited to their locality, and they may act only when they are summoned to act on behalf of those who are related to them. They may be consulted for any reason; however, some gods have specific functions and power. Some can give rain, children, prosperity, good harvest, protection, and such.

The Supreme Being is described as *ommpe utsem mbua atsen*, meaning, "he is slow to anger." Nevertheless, the gods are swift to bring punishment to people. Ironically, the rewards they give to people may not be retributive, but their punishment is. If a particular individual breaks their law, they may not only punish that individual, but also that individual's immediate and extended family, the community, and even the whole tribe. For exam-ple, I remember my granduncle was said to have been cursed by *Obrakyere Nyame* — the god of *Obrakyere*. The extended family was required to perform purification rites in order to stop the god from extending the punishment to every individual not only living but yet unborn.

Many people carry replicas, charms, and amulets from their gods for protection, and also to remind them of the gods' presence. Sacrifices are made to the gods to appease them.

Apart from the gods, there are hosts of spirits hovering around the universe. There are good spirits and bad spirits. Many Akans, and many other Africans as well, are afraid of the power of evil spirits, particularly witches. Witches are persons who possess evil spirits, which they use to harm others no matter who the person is. Some believe that witches only harm people from their own extended families. In order for another witch to be able to attack you, permission must be granted by a witch from your own family. Witches can sap the intelligence of a student, drain the wealth of the rich, cripple the plans of the wise, and destroy the energy of the healthy. They are believed to have powers that enable them to alter their human body and travel anywhere around the world to perform their clandestine activities. Witches hate to see people progress in any area of life and are particularly jealous of the rich and famous. To ward off the powers of evil spirits and witches, many people consult diviners, witch doctors, priests, and other spiritual practitioners for protection.

An important aspect of the social structure of the Akan and almost all African communities is the role ancestors play. Ancestors are the "living-dead," who have successfully completed their roles in this life. Not all dead people qualify as ancestors, only those who have lived an exemplary life worthy of emulation. The person must have made a positive contribution to the well-being of the extended family, community, or tribe. Ancestors are held in high esteem. They are the custodians of the laws and ethics that guide and protect the community. People are careful to uphold laws and taboos set for the veneration of ancestors. In all social ceremonies their presence is invoked through the pouring of libation. The *Ashantis*, for example, have the *Adae* festivals, through which they visit the stool house of ancestors and perform rites calling for the protection and guidance of the ancestors. As a child I always saw my grandmother drop a morsel of her food on the ground before she would eat. She never entirely extinguished the fire in the coal pot. She poured libation using water almost every morning. She believed her ancestors were ever-present with the living (see Rattray 1959).

Most children are named after ancestors because of the belief that when children are named after people they take on their characteristics. The ancestors are like a great crowd of witnesses watching over what the living do. They can, therefore, reward or punish people for their actions. In the case of my granduncle, cited above, apart from the *Obrakyere Nyame* punishing him, it was also believed that the ancestors were angry with him for being an irresponsible *Ebusua Panyin* (head of the family). He was required as *Ebusua Panyin* to take good care of the family property, not only for the living but for the yet unborn. They depended on him to bring unity among family members and settle any differences that arose among them. Since he was not doing that, their indignation rose against him and they joined with *Obrakyere Nyame* to punish him. The ancestors are able to provide children to the barren, assure a good harvest, reveal the cause of calamities, and provide cures and answers to problems.

THE INDIVIDUAL IN RELATIONSHIPS

Pobee (1979) writes:

Sociologists have long pointed out that while Descartes philosophized *cogito ergo sum*, the Akan society would rather argue *Cognatus ergo sum*, i.e., I belong by blood relationship, therefore, I am. In other words, in Akan society, a man fully realizes himself as a man belonging to a society. There is meaning and purpose to his life only because he belongs to a family, a clan and a tribe (p. 49).

The Supreme Being has many names, the most popular being *Nyame* and *Onyankopon*. The Akans believe that human beings are made of the elements from *Nyame*, the Supreme Being, the mother, and the father. The *Mogya*, or "blood from the mother," makes the individual a biological being. From the father, the individual receives the *Sunsum* (Spirit). The *Sunsum* is the aspect that gives an individual personality. There is no life without the seal of the Supreme Being, which is the *okra* (soul).

The Akan belong by birth to two distinct kinship groups. There are seven *Mogya* or "Blood" clans known as *Ebusua*. Each individual belongs to one of these *Ebusua* groups, which is determined through the mother. It must be emphasized that the woman alone can transmit the *Mogya*, which gives the individual the right to belong to a particular *Ebusua*.

The *Ebusua* is an extended family system in which all members see themselves as blood relations. One could travel from the south of Ghana Fanteland and go north to Asuantseland and still be considered a member of the *Ebusua* there and hold the same totem.

Through the father the individual belongs to the *Ntoro* group. This group is still maintained in places where they have *Asofo* groups. *Asofo* groups were military groups in the olden days.

Through the *okra* (soul), given by the Supreme Being, the individual receives his or her destiny. There is the belief that before the individual is born the Supreme Being gives the person the free will to choose his or her destiny. The *destiny* dictates the type of life that person wants to live. From birth, some are destined to be rich or poor, healthy or sick, chiefs or servants. Rev. Dr. Kwasi Sarpong, the present chairman of the Catholic Bishops Conference in Ghana, has asserted elsewhere that destiny to the Akan is a post-event invocation of the Akan. When everything goes on well, it is not *destiny*, but when events do not go as the Akan anticipates, it is *destiny*.

There are diviners and medicine men who are believed to have the ability to change the bad *destiny* of people through certain ceremonies and rituals. Let me underline again that the Akan sees his or her worth as an individual as he or she contributes to the well-being of the extended family. Uncles and aunts are required to take care not only of their children but of their nieces and nephews who continue to maintain the *Ebusua* lineage. Children have the responsibility to maintain uncles and aunts as well as their own parents. Everybody has the responsibility of maintaining the family, both *Ebusua* and *ntoro* cults, rites, ceremonies, ties, secrets, and so on. One irresponsible family member could bring a curse to the lineage as a whole. All things belonging to one person are held in trust for the not yet born, the living, and the living-dead (ancestors).

The Western idea of uncles, aunts, first cousins, second cousins, and so on is an infiltration into the Akan family systems. In my own family system, I do not distinguish between my parents and their brothers and sisters or cousins, nor do I distinguish between my biological siblings and cousins. For example, all my maternal aunts are my mothers, and I address them as such. I also address my cousins, no matter what degree they are, as brothers and sisters. Day (1985) suggests rightly that:

> American values emphasize youth, progress, achievement, power, perfection, planning, and efficiency. African values emphasize affiliation, collectivity, and/or obedience to authority, belief in spirituality, and acceptance of fate (subjugation to nature), and pasttime (as seen in ancestor worship and respect for the elderly) (p. 25).

To strengthen the sense of belonging and community, all stages of the individual's life—birth, puberty, adolescence, marriage, death—are marked with communal celebrations.

RITES OF PASSAGE

Birth rites begin from conception. Many Africans who have been barren for a long time consult native doctors or religious priests, including Christian and native priests, to help them have children. Some children are believed to be the offspring of spirits or gods. When such children are born, they may be given a name from the shrine of the particular god who produced him or her or may even be given a circumstantial name. Parents and families of such children are required to perform certain rites periodically to appease the god. Failure to perform such rites may result in a lot of calamities for the individual or the family. Twins are a typical example of such children. There are instances when people who have traveled far from home go back to sacrifice to the gods to ward off bad luck.

From eight days after birth, rites are performed and the child is named. Oracles, diviners, ancestors, or old people are consulted to find out which of the ancestors has been reincarnated if the child is not from a god. If no reincarnation is established, the oldest member of the extended family provides a name for the child. Normally, children are named after ancestors. Prayers are said invoking the Supreme Being, the gods and ancestors to be present and shower their blessings on the child. Africans believe that people take up the characteristics of the person after whom they were named. With the Akan in Ghana, two glasses, one with water and the other with gin, are placed in the midst of the people gathered. Three drops of water and gin are dropped on the child's tongue with the saying, "If you say it's water, let it be water; if it is gin, let it be gin." This symbolizes that the child's yes should be yes and no should be no. Names reflect the feelings of the parents, the circumstances of birth, or the time of birth.

Names for the African are very important, and the naming ceremony itself is a rite of incorporation into the extended family as well as the community, which includes the yet unborn, the living, and the living-dead (ancestors). Individuals and families present gifts to denote their acceptance of the child into the community. In some societies the child is held and shown to the skies to indicate his or her identity with the spiritual world and nature. Children are normally given names by their father's family; if a child is not named by that family, it means the child is without a father.

Puberty rites are celebrated in almost all African societies. They are occasions that mark the adolescent's development into adulthood. There are different types of puberty rites. Some are to initiate adolescents into totemic groups or secret societies. Certain teachings about the tribe and the extended family concerning their history and traditions are taught to them as well as their roles in the community. The moral laws and taboos are also inculcated in them, and more important, they are given lessons about marriage and parenthood. This rite is also a community affair. The celebration, with its communal meal, renews the ties that bind the community.

Marriage rites are perhaps the most important of all the transitional rites. Marriage helps to bring four families together (the paternal and maternal families of the couple). For the African, marriage is seen as a sacred obligation to all normal human beings. Failure on the part of any adult to marry is to stop human life — an attempt to diminish humankind on earth, which, is a major offense in the eyes of the society (Mbiti 1969a). Adults of marriageable age who are not married are social misfits. They are not given responsible positions, and their advice is not taken seriously.

A man is required to pay a dowry to the family of the woman he wants to marry. By paying the dowry, the man and his extended family are promising to take good care of the woman. The dowry is a seal to the social contract. All families and friends who receive some of the dowry become living witnesses to the marriage covenant. The Akans of Ghana always remind women who enter into marriage that when they get wealth they should bring it home to their family, but when they incur any debt they should give it to the husband to pay.

Akans who live outside their community may marry according to the laws of the land in which they live, but if they have not paid the dowry or performed the customary rites according to the requirements of their culture, their people see that marriage as null and void. It is recognized as concubinage.

Kofi met Efua in the United States and got married without getting the blessings of their families. Kofi did not perform any customary rite on behalf of Efua. Efua got cancer and died, and Kofi took her body back to Ghana. Efua's family was informed of her death and was expected to meet the body at the airport, but the family did not. They sent a message to Kofi's family that they had heard somebody from Kofi's family had lived illegally with their daughter in the United States. When their daughter was sick, Kofi did not have the courtesy to inform them. Now their daughter is dead, and they have heard rumors that her body is being sent to Ghana by that "stranger" (Kofi). Efua's family will hold Kofi's family responsible for allowing Kofi to live with Efua without performing the marriage rite, which then resulted in Efua's death. Kofi's family has to sacrifice to pacify Efua's family. They will perform the marriage rite before they recognize Kofi as their in-law and widower.

The main aim of marriage is to procreate new members of the community. Childlessness is looked upon with scorn. It is one of the important grounds for divorce. Married couples are encouraged to get a divorce if after maybe three years of marriage, they don't produce a child. Most often women are blamed as barren and not men. Childless women who choose to stay in their marriages, often encourage their husbands to marry other women to have children, thus encouraging polygamy. Men also use childlessness as an excuse to marry more than one woman. Since children are the seal and glory of marriage, it is very difficult to break up a marriage with children. Children add to the social prestige of the family. Boys and girls have different importance in the family, according to their family line of inheritance. In matriarchal systems, girls born into the family are more important than boys, because when a boy grows to have children, his children will not be members of his family, but of his wife's. Because of this, most fathers in maternal family systems are not very responsible to their children. It is the duty of the wife's brothers to be responsible for her children. This brings an extra burden to the uncles if they have children of their own. This does not mean, however, that fathers are irresponsible toward their children.

Jojo was married to his wife Nana for thirty years. They had five children in the marriage. Jojo died suddenly through an accident. His wife and children were ejected from their home by Jojo's family because Jojo's children belong to his wife's family. They also confiscated everything that Jojo had.

In such circumstances, wives and children are protected if the husband wrote a will before his death. In spite of people preparing wills, there are sometimes litigations on some of the property of the husbands.

Western society insists on monogamous fidelity, while African ethics allow polygamy. The African may have a society wedding with all its legal implications but might not see anything wrong with marrying other women and having children with the other wife.

Death is also seen as transitional and a continuation of life here on earth. To the African, nothing happens without a cause. Death may have a physical cause, but the African will always go beyond the physical to find spiritual causes. Death may come through the breaking of a taboo or oath or being cursed. People also believe that an enemy may have used witchcraft, sorcery, or evil magic to cause death.

There are elaborate funeral rites, not only for the deceased, but also for the widow or widower. The rites for the dead are performed in order for the dead to have a smooth separation from this world and transition to continue life with the ancestors. There is a belief that if the rites are not performed correctly, the dead may continue to hover around this world and haunt people. Those responsible for the rites are careful to do whatever is expected in order not to incur the displeasure of the dead. Since the dead are now spirits, they can reward or punish. Prayers are said to them to punish those who may have been the cause of their death and reward those who love them with children and prosperity.

As part of the grieving process, widows, widowers, and children of the deceased go through rites of absolution and purification to save them from the enemy who killed the person and to have physical, spiritual, and emotional separation from the deceased. Children are required to be present at the funerals of their parents, uncles, aunts, and grandparents except in extreme circumstances. Those who live abroad and are not able to attend the funerals experience a lot of guilt and shame. However, they perform funeral rites wherever they reside. Mpolo and Kalu (1985) underline the importance of the extended family system:

> The extended family structure provides mechanisms which reduce stress and share whatever guilt feelings which might arise due to personal or intrafamilial conflicts. The existence of a set of rules which regulated individual behaviors and helped the individual to pass smoothly from one life cycle to another with a sense of emotional security . . . (p. 105).

AKAN CONCEPTS OF CAUSATION OF PROBLEMS

Most African people see the individual as a psychosomatic whole comprising body, soul, and spirit. As mentioned earlier, every human being has a spirit—*Ntoro*—derived from the father, and this spirit is the life force of a person. The *Ntoro* connects the person to his or her ancestral lineage. From the mother the individual receives the blood—*Mogya*—which gives the person a bodily identity. People from the same maternal lineage are blood relatives—*Ebusua*. From the Supreme Being, the individual receives the *Kra*, the soul. The *Kra* is the life force, which makes the individual a living being. When the Supreme Being takes away the *Kra*, a person loses his or her life.

The Akans believe that before a person is born into the world of the living, that person bargains with the Supreme Being about the type of *Kra* he or she wants to be. Whatever happens to an individual happens because of the type of *Kra* the person has. For example, if a person is doing well in business, it may be attributed to his good *Kra*. Conversely, if things go wrong it may be due to that person's bad *Kra*.

Before undertaking major issues in life Akans often consult with diviners to find out what type of *Kra* they possess. This determines the person's destiny, which can be changed through rituals, sacrifices, and purifications.

There is also the belief that nothing happens to the individual by chance or accident. Kofi had a car accident on his way to his uncle's funeral. When the diviner was consulted, he suggested that Kofi's accident was caused by his uncle's wife, who wanted Kofi to die because he was going to be his uncle's heir.

Even though sickness, death, and natural catastrophes are inevitable parts of our existence, they are seen as intrusions in life and therefore unnatural. Attempts are made through divination to understand them and find remedies for them.

The Akans of Ghana, like most African communities, differentiate between two kinds of sickness. Some sickness may be *soryarba* or "spiritual illness," and cannot be treated without ritual purifications and sacrifices. The other kind of sickness, which is seen as "natural illness," may be treated with modern Western medicine or traditional African medicine. The people usually consult with diviners to be certain there are no spiritual causes for the illness.

Many African societies have communal or tribal taboos and moral and ethical laws. A breach of these may bring disequilibrium to the person who broke them and his or her family and perhaps the entire community. "The fathers may eat sour grapes and the children's teeth may be set on edge." People believe that the rewards and punishment of one generation may be passed on from generation to generation.

A man committed incest against his stepchild at the seashore. That particular area was believed also to be the residence of a god. Unfortunately, during this time the fishermen of the vicinity were experiencing a bad harvest. The offender was not only reprimanded for breaking the taboo of the society but also for infuriating the gods. The punishment—the poor fishing harvest—affected the whole community. He was not the only one required to pacify the gods in order to neutralize the consequences of his action; the onus fell on the whole community.

In the case of my granduncle, cited above, when he became the family head, he held every property of the extended family in trust for the living, the dead, and the yet unborn. By embezzling the proceeds from the sale of family property, he broke a moral law, and the ancestors agreed with *Obrakyere Nyame* to punish him.

TRADITIONAL COUNSELORS AND THERAPIES

Traditionally, the deeply troubled are counseled in diverse and complex ways. It must also be noted that counseling in the Akan society is not only done when people have problems but also as "preventive counseling." From pregnancy through initiation rites of birth, puberty, marriage, and death, individuals and groups are counseled on "how to's" in order to prevent calamities. For example, during puberty ceremonies girls are sometimes confined for about a week and educated on how to be good housewives, parents, sexual partners, and so on. In every stage of the individual's life there are specialists in the community who are consulted.

When there are problems to be resolved, normally there are family councils. Members of these councils are respected in society and regarded as people who have good morals and are wise. With the Akan, the individual's problem affects his or her immediate and extended family, including the yet unborn and the living-dead. By virtue of their age and social status, some individuals are vested with authority to hold a juristic status in the family council. All *ebusuapanyin* (heads of extended families) have the right and duty to perform the service of moderator in a family council. The ancestors look to this person as the mentor and restorer of order and peace in the family. He or she is accountable to the ancestors and to the living and yet unborn for faithful exercise of this authority. Whoever becomes the moderator of the family council can ask for the help of neighbors, kinspeople, or friends to serve as jurors. The jurors are not expected to find who is guilty or not guilty (even though this is part of their duties), but they are required to help settle differences and bring social equilibrium.

Because the ancestors are the ultimate and superior authorities in the family group, family councils always begin with a libation invoking their presence and asking them for wisdom.

Those who are found to have erred are asked to pacify the innocent. All present may drink or sip from the same drinking cup of an alcoholic beverage to signify that they are witnesses to the settlement. In some cases a communal meal is served.

A pivotal aspect of counseling in the Akan culture is divination. As Pobee (1979) suggests, the Akan has a religious ontology. For the Akan, whatever an individual experiences physically might have a religious dimension. Divination is therefore seen as a fundamental tool in diagnosing the supernatural causes of the problem and the course of treatment.

Diviners are believed to have perceptions into the unknown including the spirit world, the unseen, and the future. They also have an understanding of the laws of nature that bring disequilibrium or equilibrium to individuals and the whole community.

> The diviner's task is the practical one of disclosing the causes of misfortune and death. His job is not to foretell the future but rather to scrutinize the past in order to identify the spiritual and human agents responsible for personal misfortunes. Since all human problems such as infertility, illness, and trouble in hunting are ascribed to moral conflicts within the human community, the diviner's task is to disclose acts of immorality which have provoked the vengeance of the ancestors and to reveal the destructive hands of witches (Ray 1976, 104).

Through oracular diagnosis, the diviners prescribe treatment, which can be as simple as giving alms, wearing an amulet, or taking a ritual bath, or more elaborate, like communal sacrifice.

I come from a fishing town. In a particular year, fishermen had a poor catch, which affected the living standard of the whole town. A diviner was consulted, who suggested that the gods and the ancestors were displeased with the people. The only way the gods and ancestors could be appeased was by a communal sacrifice of a cow. A white cow was gorgeously adorned with gold and silver ornaments and led through the principal streets of the town. The cow was sacrificed at midnight on the sea and part of its meat cooked for a communal meal. All members of the community were expected to be part of the ceremony, since it affected the whole society.

Diviners are believed to be agents and mouthpieces of spirits or gods. These spirits or gods possess them when they are divining. Their countenances and voices and mannerisms may change when they are possessed. It is sometimes difficult to distinguish between priests, who serve the gods, and diviners. Priests have symbolic authority because they are the go-betweens for humans and gods. Priests interpret the gods, so they are also consulted when there are problems that may be ascribed to the gods. They have a powerful leadership role in the Akan Society. Priests may operate as diviners and also prescribe herbal medicines for curing disease.

The Akan adage "Opanyin nnyi wo fie a due," meaning, "If you do not have any elder or older person in your house, you are in trouble," is indicative of the responsibility of family elders to counsel people. Old age is always equated with wisdom, therefore people go to the elderly (senior citizens) for counsel. When any individual misbehaves in public or has a bad character, older relatives are blamed for it. People normally go to senior citizens, who are the receptors of wisdom, for *advice*. Note that I have emphasized *advice*. Giving advice is an essential ingredient in counseling with the Akan.

All towns and villages have their own chief, a position which is hereditary. The chiefs, *ebusua*, are regarded as the people who first settled in the area. By right of birth and ancestry they "own" the community and everything in the community. Chiefs have elders in different areas in the town or village who are heads of their own areas. They are accountable to the chief.

Chiefs have their own councils, which include all the elders of the town or village and others who are coopted by the chief. They also form a family court/council to settle cases in the community. Busia and Forde (1970) summarize the role of the chief:

> The most important aspect of Ashante chieftaincy was undoubtedly the religious one. The Ashante chief fulfilled a sacral role. His stool, the symbol of his office, was a sacral emblem. It represented the community, their solidarity, their permanence, the continuity. The chief was the link between the living and dead and his highest role was when he affiliated in the public religious roles which gave expression to the community values. He then acted as the representative of the community, whose members are believed to include those who are stillborn. The sacral aspect of the chief's role was a powerful sanction of the chief's authority (p. 190).

I suggest strongly that this sacral role of the chief in the Ashante society has been transferred as part of the pastoral authority of the pastor, priest, prophet, of the Christian church. With the advent of Christianity, the church has taken an important role in dealing with issues in life through its representatives. This pastoral authority includes the right to do pastoral counseling in the community.

DOING PASTORAL COUNSELING WITH THE AKAN

A working definition of pastoral counseling may give a sound base for understanding the work of the pastoral counselor with the Akan. Lartey (1987) gives a definition of pastoral counseling that explains my basic concept of pastoral counseling in Africa. He refers to pastoral counseling as:

> A helping activity undertaken by people who recognize a spiritual or religious dimension to life, which by the use of verbal or non-verbal, direct or indirect, literal or symbolic modes of communication, aims at preventing or relieving the anxieties of persons and fostering their growth as fully functioning human beings and the development of a society in which all persons can live a human life (p. 115).

I contend that in all pastoral relationships there is an encounter with the existential question, How can a person know God in such a way as to make sense of life? This existential question extends to our relations with the whole of creation, both physical and spiritual, and affects our interpersonal and intra-personal relationships.

Karl Barth (1963) posits that Christian theology fails to make visible the decisive dimension of God as the God of human beings. He suggests that it would be better to speak of God in "theo-anthropology," that is, God as the God of the people. Firet (1986) stretches Barth's position a little further. He writes:

> Theology is not only the study of the knowledge of God, it is also the study of the process of getting to know God, of the events which happen between God and human beings and between persons, with a view to the process of getting to know, and knowing God, functions of His revelation and his companionship with us as human beings, including the functioning of the faith community pastoral role fulfillment and pastoral communication (p. 12).

It is my belief that God's self-revelation to people takes place through the history of the people. God is concerned with people in their history and uses their modes of understanding to reveal God's own active history with them. These may include their myths, symbols, language, rites — in short, God uses *their* culture.

Christianity came to Africa in the garb of Western culture. "Throughout the history of missions, it has long practiced a 'deculturization' control over African populations — forcing them brutally to sever their roots and lose their authenticity" (Ela 1988, 24). There was an assault on whatever was African that the missionaries did not understand.

> The missionary enterprise among the Akans ... being Western in outlook and emphasis, felt bound to deny the Akan worldview, not only on the basis of what was essentially Christian belief, but on the ground of what was, in effect, a European view (Williamson 1974, 168).

For example, to be Christian was to have a Western name. People with traditional names had their names changed when they were baptized, taking away the historical realities of the circumstances of their birth. Drumming and dancing, which are used therapeutically in certain circumstances in African culture, were banned or slighted. Commenting on the value of African religious beliefs and practices for Christian theology, Mercy Amba Oduyeye observes that "it is evident that the missionary religions, together with modern technology, have proved inadequate to our needs" (in Appiah-Kubi and Torres 1979).

A theological foundation for pastoral counseling with the Akan must take into serious consideration the Akans' culture. In recent times there has been a long debate over whether to Africanize Christianity or Christianize Africa. I do not intend to do a lengthy theological analysis of pastoral counseling, but I dare suggest that "whatsoever is noble [in the Akan culture], whatsoever is right [in the Akan culture], whatsoever is pure [in the Akan culture], whatsoever is lovely [in the Akan culture], whatsoever is admirable [in the Akan culture], if anything is excellent or praiseworthy [in the Akan culture], think about such things [and use them for the good of the Akan]" (Philippians 4:8, with phrases in parenthesis mine).

My theological viewpoint is that in God's general revelation, God revealed God's self to the Akan, hence the Akan's belief in the Supreme Being who created the universe. However, pastoral counselors must interpret in concrete terms God's special revelation and covenant relation with all people and all creation in the "incarnation event" of Jesus Christ, who brings *salvation* to all. Salvation for the Akan is *Ahoto*. Hood (1990) explains vividly what this *Ahoto* means in African concept:

> Salvation—carries with it the idea of empowerment as well as deliverance, rescue from powerless or helpless situation to one of potency or power, gained through purification rites. ... Generally there are three major situations or forces by which the African seeks salvation and deliverance: 1) daily hardships, such as crop failure due to the weather, everyday conflicts, infant mortality, and female infertility; 2) evil spirits, forces and persons, such as witches and sorcerers; 3) lack of good relationship with ancestral spirits and divinities (p. 114).

It is therefore imperative in pastoral counseling that an impression is not given that salvation in Jesus Christ is only being delivered from the pangs of sin and turning one's world view from being an Akan to being a Westerner as conveyed by missionary Christianity.

Imasogie (1983) calls for a new emphasis in the role of the Holy Spirit in the church and with individuals. He suggests that the African has more faith in spiritual guidance than psychological guidance. The rise and rapid growth of "Spiritual churches" in Africa give credence to his suggestion. The Spiritual churches, by emphasizing the power of the Holy Spirit in the struggles of life, have brought a new dimension to African Christianity. The Holy Spirit is God at work in the world, creating, recreating, and unfolding the truth about the incarnation. The Holy Spirit bestows various gifts—prophecy, teaching, healing, preaching, and so on—but above all, love for the brokenhearted. Through the Holy Spirit, God in Jesus Christ has built a new community—the church—to be God's presence in the world.

Pastoral counseling is a participation in the ministry of Jesus Christ, who is the unique presence of God. Jesus Christ is the source and pattern of the church's ministry. His life, death, and resurrection are a reconciling of

God with the deeply troubled. Anderson (1979), based on John 16:7-15, sums up this ministry in these words:

> All ministry is Christ's ministry of faithfulness to the Father on behalf of the world. The sending of the Holy Spirit continues this ministry; it does not constitute the creation of another ministry (p. 20).

Pastoral counseling is the ministry of the whole church, for both lay and clergy. I have suggested above that the authority of the chief as described by Busia has somehow been transferred to the church leader, that is, the minister, priest, prophet. As a sacral authority one important aspect of his duties is to help to bring social harmony among individuals and others. But the chief does not attempt to do this alone; he or she uses the elders.

A head of family does not attempt to deal with problems in the *Ebusua* without summoning others to help. Fortunately, most of the churches in Ghana have a system in which elders are used. For example, the Methodists have class leaders and the Presbyterians have presbyters and the Church of the Pentecost has elders. I propose that such people, including those who are identified as having the gifts and graces to do pastoral counseling, be trained and empowered for this ministry within the churches.

Let me use the definition of pastoral counseling by Lartey, quoted above, to summarize the task:

1. Pastoral counseling is an activity undertaken by people.

I suggest that for this activity to be successful, the people who undertake it should have some training about the world view of the African.

2. Pastoral counseling recognizes a spiritual or religious dimension to life.

The pastoral counselor should take into serious consideration the religious world view of the client, no matter how trivial or stupid it might seem to the pastoral counselor. With the Akan society, the causation of disease or problem may have a religious ontology.

3. By the use of verbal or non-verbal, direct or indirect, literal or symbolic modes of communication, the pastoral counselor aims at preventing or relieving the anxieties of persons.

An understanding of the symbolic language of clients and the community is important. These may include proverbs, myths, stories, dreams, rituals, and so forth.

4. Pastoral counseling fosters the clients' growth as fully functioning human beings and the development of a society in which all persons can live a human life.

Being able to live in harmony with oneself is to be a part of the society. Akans find their humanness when they live in consonance with the morals of the society and live for others. A departure from family and its norms may cause problems. It is the task of pastoral counseling to help people relate well to one another.

MY EMERGING ORIENTATION

I find some concepts in family systems and Adlerian counseling helpful for counseling with Africans. I am trying to graft some of these concepts onto the African culture.

Basic to Adler's theory is that each individual is a part of a social community. The individual's sense of self is a function of the person's social identity. All individuals have the primary need to feel belonging and to have a place in the social community. Fundamentally, the need to belong binds humans together. The sense of belonging to the community is what the German word *gemeinschaftsgefuhl* describes: "a feeling for the community that also implies a feeling with a sense of oneness with the community" (Ferguson 1984, 5). *Gemeinschaftsgefuhl* translated as "social interest" is the identification and willingness of the individual to live for the common good of the community. According to Adler, social interest is both innate and potential in every person, but interaction with the community helps it to grow. Only those who are willing to contribute to the common good of the community without thought of reward can feel satisfied with themselves and their lives. The crucial questions to be asked are: "Have the rules of the community life been observed? Is the individual ready to subordinate himself to them?" (Dreikurs 1950).

Adlerians point out that the world view of the child and a sense of who he or she is, is based on early social experiences. It is in the context of the group that the child finds a sense of identity. It is when the child feels an important part of the group that the child contributes to the group welfare. As the individual grows older and expands personal relationships he or she continues to learn from life experiences to deal with problems.

I find the Adlerian idea of social interest important for me as an African counselor. As already stated, the African life is intrinsically communal. An individual finds fullness as a human being only in his or her relationship and contribution to the common good of the community. The concept of individual success or failure, therefore, is secondary. The ethnic group, the village, the locality are crucial in one's estimation of oneself. We can truly know ourselves if we remain true to our community (Appiah-Kubi and Torres 1979). Sometimes when people have problems in life they think it is because they have denied their community and their contribution to the community. It is only when such people have pacified the community that they have equilibrium in their lives.

FAMILY INFLUENCES

Adler's theory is that the early years of a child's interaction with the family are crucial to the well-being of the child. Those early years influence what the person does in adult life. This goes back to prenatal and perinatal periods. Perinatal describes the critical period just before, during, and immediately following birth (Dinkmeyer, Dinkmeyer, and Sperry 1987, 27).

This concept is very important in African culture. A child may be named or given a birthmark depending on what happened to the mother, father, or an important person in the family when the mother was pregnant. For example, a child may be given two marks on the cheek immediately after he or she is born because the mother fell sick while pregnant and believed it was an attempt by evil spirits to kill the baby. A child whose mother dies after he or she is born may be given a name that explains the circumstances of the mother's death. In counseling, I ask clients to tell stories surrounding their mother's pregnancy.

BIRTH ORDER

Birth order in Adlerian counseling is very significant. It provides probability of the types of experiences the client had and their influence on the individual's personality development. Birth order, however, does not predict the personality type of the individual:

Birth order then must be explained dynamically by taking into consideration how much the child influences the other members of the family and how they influence him. . . . With the birth of each child, the situation, and therefore, the environment change because 1) the parents are older and more experienced or more discouraged; 2) the parents may be more prosperous; 3) the parents may have moved to another neighborhood; 4) because of divorce or death, there may be stepparents (Dinkmeyer, Kinkmeyer, and Sperry 1987, 27).

In many African societies the oldest male is responsible for the upkeep of his parents when they are old. In matriarchal societies uncles take care of their nieces and nephews. In many cases, particularly with people who try to adopt the Western type of nuclear family, they decide to shirk their responsibilities; this brings discord in their marriage and extended families.

THE FAMILY CONSTELLATION

Adlerians see the family as a dynamic whole. The family constellation questionnaire helps to bring into focus the dynamics in the family. This may include grandparents, aunts, uncles, maids, sex, age, socio-economic status, peers, family values, "who was who," adjustments to social and physical problems, and so forth.

Many Africans do not read nor write. Even those who do read and write are not used to filling out long questionnaires. The way to solicit the information from the questionnaire is to do it orally.

THE MULTI-GENERATIONAL TRANSMISSION PROCESS

To get more insight into the family constellation, I use some of the concepts of the inter-generational theory of Murray Bowen. Bowen was convinced that the family of origin is the key to family therapy. Bowen also believed that through the multi-generational transmission process, families hand down family traditions, values, symptoms, and so on:

> The more differentiated and healthy the family process, the more variations there will be in persons and generations; the less differentiated the more pronounced will be the fixed patterns, the repetitions scripting of lives . . . from generation to generation (Augsburger 1986, 185).

Bowen is known for the use of the genogram for taking the family history and understanding family connections. Bowen's main aim in therapy is to help the individual to differentiate from the group.

African family traditions are handed down from generation to generation as described by Bowen. Children are even named after their ancestors. Some types of professions and traits are carried on from generation to generation. I use Bowen's tool, the genogram, to help clients gain insight into their family traditions and develop an awareness of the individual's identity in relation to that of the group. This is in contrast to Bowen's goal of helping individuation of the client. The interdependency and cohesion of the individual to the family or kinship group takes precedence over individuation. Insisting on individuation of the individual while using Bowen's inter-generational theory with the African would be detrimental.

LIFESTYLE AND EARLY RECOLLECTIONS COUNSELING

For Adlerians, early recollections are important in understanding a person's lifestyle. Before the age of eight, a child develops certain characteristics and ideas from events that occurred in the child's life. Character is, therefore, simply a manifestation of a certain plan which the child has evolved and to which he or she will adhere throughout the rest of his or her life (Dreikurs 1950). The individual develops his or her lifestyle from his or her life plan. Individuals have biased standpoints from early experiences and use such biases to justify events or behaviors.

The goal in soliciting early recollections and lifestyle is not necessarily to change the lifestyle of the individual or predict the individual's behavior, but to understand the individual and to help him or her (Dinkmeyer, Dinkmeyer, and Sperry 1987).

THE FAMILY COUNCIL

I have been emphasizing the place of the family and community in the individual's life in Africa. Life is only life in community (Appiah-Kubi and Torres 1979). The family is the *summum bonum* of African lifestyle and ethics. It is, therefore, imperative at one point or the other to involve the family in therapy. As already said, a family member may not be a blood relative, but people who have been *in loco parentis* for the individual may sometimes be more than biological relatives. In my own life, I have people I call mothers, fathers, uncles, who are not biologically related to me. My own parents consult them on issues concerning me.

In the family council the counselor may invite elders, whom the client respects, to meet. The counselor is part of the group, but more the moderator.

The family council almost always begins with the ritual of prayer and the pouring of libation invoking the presence of the ancestors, the yet unborn and the good spirits of the society.

The client tells his or her story to the council. With insights gained at individual sessions, the counselor may come in and interject his or her observation. The client, after telling the story, leaves the group for a while to allow them to deliberate on what they have heard, to make observations, and to put forth recommendations.

The Akan finds healing and wholeness only in reconciliation with others and the spiritual world. A society is in equilibrium when its customs are maintained, its goals attained, and the spirit powers given regular and adequate recognition (Dickson 1984). Healing and wholeness of the individual in distress may involve some rites recommended by the family council. Some of the rites are standard. There are some that may have alternatives. Depending on the individual's beliefs, the counselor may lead the individual to bargain for alternatives. Let me illustrate the above with the story of Aba, which is also a typical example of the questions Africans ask when they have problems; that is, Who or what is the cause of my problem? Why now?

Aba came to the United States in the late seventies to read for a Master's degree in psychiatric nursing. During the course of studies her husband married another woman. Aba thought because she was the legally wedded wife, the other woman was only a concubine. She believed her husband married this other woman because she was far away. However, after her second year in school, she went to Ghana for holidays and was shocked to hear from her husband that he no longer intended to be married to her. Aba came back to the United States to continue her studies. According to her, everything was all right with her in the United States. She had her degree, a good job, bought a house, and remarried. She had two children, who were living in Ghana. She applied to the immigration department to bring them to the United States and succeeded. However, when the children joined her, things began to change. She was sick for a while; her husband's attitude toward her changed for the worse; her children were truant in school and very disobedient.

Aba came for counseling with her children. Her husband did not join them because he felt going to any type of counseling indicates mental illness—which is typical of many Africans. Aba gained insight into some of her problems, but also believed that there could be an "outside agent" causing all these things. Aba wrote to her brother about her problems. In his reply, her brother also complained about bad events in his life. As counseling progressed, Aba reported that she was a twin sister to her brother. Aba's tribe in Ghana, the Akans, believe that all twins are children of spirits. Annually, there should be a feast to thank the spirits and ask for their guidance.

Missionary Christianity suggested that such rites are idolatry. However, some churches and families have introduced rites to replace the traditional rites. Aba's family adopted the Christian rite and performed it annually until she went to college. Aba felt her problems were partly due to not performing the rite, a betrayal of spirits who had been helping her succeed in life. Aba decided to go to Ghana for the rite.

There was a family gathering, libation was poured, and a feast followed. Members of Aba's extended family found relief because some believed the punishment and calamity of the twins—Aba and her brother—would have been visited on them. The rite and the family gathering provided a psychological avenue of relief from their fears. Aba once again felt that she was reconciled with her family.

RITUALS, SYMBOLS, AND SYMBOLIC LANGUAGE IN COUNSELING

Akans use symbols and symbolic language to express their experience in everyday life. A visitor to any African country may wonder why all public transportation vehicles have statements written on them. These statements depict the innermost feelings of the persons who write them.

This symbolic language is an important tool in counseling with the Akan. The symbolic language may include myths, stories, proverbs, metaphors, music, and others. Mpolo and Kalu (1985) suggest:

Doing pastoral counseling means becoming aware of and, whenever appropriate, incorporating into the therapeutic process myths and symbols found in the assumptive and cultural world of the individual or group of individuals seeking counseling (p. 114).

In the case of Aba, cited above, she suggested that she was like a he goat. When I asked her to explain further what she meant by that, she said the goat has a very bad odor and nobody likes the goat to get closer because of its smell. The goat is also an ugly animal. Because of the bad odor, not many people like the meat of a goat. Aba felt that spiritually she had been turned into a goat and, therefore, when people tried to get close to her, they retreated because of her spiritual "odor of the goat."

I indicated earlier that people are also named according to the circumstances of their birth. Another important thing Aba brought up in counseling was that she was named for her grandmother, who was highly respected in society. Aba thought it was a challenge for her to emulate her grandmother. She felt she was a disgrace to her family because she was not like her grandmother.

In counseling, I encourage clients to tell stories about their lives and use their own metaphors and symbolic language to help them gain insights into their problems.

I have in recent times appreciated the value of music in African therapy. The Akans, especially the Ashantis, have different kinds of traditional music, which express different types of moods. For example, during funerals, the adowa music is played for the grieving families to dance to. Not quite ten years ago members of the Methodist church in Ghana were banned from traditional drumming and dancing because the missionaries erroneously interpreted it as idolatry. Traditionally, it is used to help grieving persons express their feelings and to help them through the grieving process. I believe music and dance therapy is an important component of pastoral counseling with the Akan society.

I have emphasized how important rites and rituals are in Akan therapy. There is no occasion in the Akan's life that is devoid of rites and rituals. As I have already suggested, the pastoral counselor should use whatever is traditionally good to help bring psychological catharsis.

The Christian church has many religious resources that can be used. These include prayers, baptism, the sacraments, hymn singing, and so on. My experience in counseling is that almost all my African clients expect me to use a religious resource, particularly prayer, before or after each session. The churches in Ghana are adopting a lot of these Christian rites to help the deeply hurt.

The Winneba Methodist Church has developed a rite for widows and widowers to help them go through the grieving process. Confirmation of adolescents is now replacing puberty rites. Unfortunately, the moral lessons adolescents are taught in traditional puberty rites are lost in the church's confirmation services.

Clinebell (1966) sounds a note of warning about the use of religious resources in counseling. He suggests that 1) they should be used sparingly, only after one is aware of the counselee's needs; 2) they should be used in such a way that they do not diminish the individual's sense of responsibility; 3) they should not be used in ways that create magical expectations or arouse guilt about them; 4) they should be used in supportive, crises, confrontational, and existential counseling, and less in insight counseling; 5) they should be used to deepen a relationship and not as a substitute for relating.

Pastoral counseling with the Akan is incomplete without moral or ethical counseling. In the discussion of causation of disease and problems, I asserted that the breaking of a taboo or social norm could be associated with disease or problems.

In 1980 I was a full-time pastor overseeing about forty congregations. I was expected to visit all of them within a period of four months. This involved a lot of walking, sometimes about fifteen to thirty miles a day. Apart from this, I had other pastoral duties, including being chaplain to schools and hospitals. The work was very stressful, and it wore me down. Just about that time, I was struggling with marital issues. I broke down and was hospitalized. Rumors circulated that I was sick because I had broken some moral principles. Unfortunately, pastors who were my friends also believed that and in their counseling encouraged me to confess and do the necessary rites in order to be healed.

There are a lot of "do's" and "don't's" in the Akan society, the breaking of which bring psychological distress to many people. I believe that a lot of *somato* forms and conversion disorders are due to the pain, guilt, and shame that accompany the breaking of social norms.

The task of the pastoral counselor is to help clients deal with the moral claims of the society and their own cognitive thoughts about it. The pastoral counselor should not be judgmental but endeavor to bring assurance of grace as found in the love of God in Christ.

Firet's (1986) comments about pastoral care summarize what I mean by the pastoral counselor assuming the office as a moral counselor. He posits:

> Pastoral care is ... an address to an equal. ... Perhaps this person has lost her way; she is flooded by a sense of inadequacy. But pastoral care means that she is addressed in the language of respect and dignity. However undignified and worthless she seems, pastoral care is primarily an acknowledgment of her in her dignity. However irresponsibly he may have lived, pastoral care is an acknowledgment of him in his freedom and responsibility, an acknowledgment which must often assume the form of helping him regain acceptance and the experience of that freedom and responsibility (p. 267).

ASIA

7

THAILAND

DANIEL BOYD

Daniel A. Boyd, M.M., Maryknoll priest working in Thailand, points out how the establishment of a counseling relationship requires the comfortable acceptance by the counselor of the role of trained professional and expert, and the ability to maintain that role differentiation throughout the counseling process. Within the parameters of a successful professional relationship, self-disclosure on the part of the professional is almost sure to be counterproductive.

Careful attention to dreams is a pre-requisite for fully entering into a client's psychic life. Probing into near-death experiences, more frequent in the Third World, is also a valuable source of information. Since most Thai people believe in ghosts and spirits, openness to the impact of spirits is important. Rev. Boyd speaks of the important role of "monkhood" in the Thai culture and the special role of astrologers and fortune tellers.

Thailand—the Land of Smiles. Many are the hours a pastoral counselor may spend wondering what is behind a smile! There are smiles of friendship, smiles of embarrassment, smiles of greeting, and general smiles of happiness, of course. The mysteries of the Orient begin the moment a client walks into your office, because the Thai smile is used to communicate a wide range of feelings and meanings.

Counseling in a cross-cultural context such as one finds in Thailand is a challenging endeavor. Thais do not generally seek out counseling, except possibly from a monk for the purpose of subduing tumultuous feelings—and this would be a single visit. The average person has no awareness of a psychotherapeutic process. Therefore, the establishment of a referral network is very important. Walk-ins just don't seem to happen. However, medical personnel are often happy to know of the availability of services of a Thai-speaking counselor, and opportunities are plentiful for offering counseling services to the English-speaking expatriate community.

We counselors are all familiar with the simple guidelines for the establishment of the typical, Western, helping relationship. Relationships in Thailand are quite different. Here, relationships always begin with the establishment of an inferior-superior status understanding. Westerners may be put off by the questions Thais ask very quickly upon meeting a stranger: "How old are you?" or "How much do you earn?" This is an attempt to establish who is "above" and who is "below" in the relationship. This will determine how future greetings are done, which pronouns can be used in address, and how the various niceties of relationship are to be undertaken.

For the counseling relationship, we do our clients justice by introducing ourselves in such a way as to establish the superior-inferior relationship from the very outset. And we don't think twice about this, regardless of our gospel values. The counselor as the trained professional is expected to assume the superior role. Anything less than this ("Let's try to be equals" or "I am here to serve you") will indeed result in early termination. It may be perceived by the client as game playing; it certainly signals a lack of cultural awareness. To the Thai mind, there would be absolutely no reason to see a counselor, much less pay one, unless he or she has some sort of wisdom or method to offer; thus the counselor is in the superior role. Counselors may introduce themselves as doctor or teacher. They establish a helping relationship by establishing themselves as the healer or teacher, or guide. This can be done with thorough honesty. In Thai culture friends do not generally burden each other with their problems, so the counselor must shed any Western notions of relating as first-name-basis equals.

Related to the superior-inferior status in the helping relationship are decisions about self-disclosure. Decisions about this are difficult in any culture, and there continues to be ongoing debate about the appropriateness and amount of self-disclosure even in our own society. While in the West we sometimes find self-disclosure to be of assistance in building the helping relationship, or in dealing with transference issues, this is very rarely the case when counseling Thais. Self-disclosure may be seen as inappropriately intimate within the framework of a professional relationship, such as the counselor-client relationship. In addition, some forms of self-disclosure will be seen as signs of weakness or lack of wisdom, which will lessen the trust level of the client. Thai clients do not seem to have the same kind of curiosity about their counselor I have encountered in the West. It would be a mistake to assume it. It would be a further mistake to assume that self-disclosure would generally do service to the helping relationship. Most of my self-disclosure takes the form of congruency; that is, admitting my lack of clarity about specific cultural concepts or puzzling about the true meaning of what a client is saying. Congruency is important, but it is different from self-disclosure.

Most of the Thai people I have come to know appreciate an easy continuum between the physical and the metaphysical, or what we may consider the normal and the paranormal. It is not uncommon for a Thai client to have had every significant event that is presently guiding or influencing his or her life of a "liminal" nature. This will generally not be revealed unless the counselor asks directly. The counselor should do so early in the counseling relationship, my own preference being for session two or three.

Dreams can be an important focus for symbolic representations and even messages. Many Thais believe that revelations about their present-day situation, or future fate, may come to them in dreams. One client, suffering from an apparent anxiety disorder, dreamed of ghosts trying to enter his bedroom. He concluded that he was living too close to a cemetery and decided to move. While his anxiety didn't disappear, it did seem that the action he took to correct his situation lessened his anxiety considerably and he started to sleep much better. While we in the West may interpret this as the client establishing control over his life's events, thus lowering his anxiety, what would the Thai client say?

Near-death experiences are more frequent in the Third World due to the number of serious illnesses contracted, especially in childhood but also later in life, and due to the higher frequency of accidents resulting from a lack of safety measures. The liminal state experienced during high fevers, for example, seems to be a time when important insights may be gained into the metaphysical world. Chai, a 32-year-old male, complained of failures in the competitive business world. He seemed unable to be assertive enough with his colleagues, although he did not appear to lack self-confidence. In relating childhood events, Chai mentioned that when he began secondary school he was very clumsy in sports and the other students used to laugh at him. He became very ill at one point and was close to death (possibly due to malaria). During a high fever he saw spirits, who strengthened him, thus effecting his recovery. After that Chai did very well at sports because of the strength he had gained in this near-death experience. In our therapy I drew on the memories of this experience, which Chai had more or less forgotten, as well as some assertiveness techniques from the West adapted to Thai requirements for politeness. Chai does much better with his colleagues now. As therapy closed, he thanked me for helping him recover the strength he had gained in his fever dream so long ago. He never mentioned the assertiveness techniques.

Most Thai people believe in ghosts. This is not meant to apply only to village farmers, but to engineers, professors, nurses, and others. It is very important to ask each client about ghosts. My own technique is simple; I say, "What about ghosts?" The answer is often enlightening. Some Thais have an awareness that many Westerners do not believe in ghosts and are afraid of being scoffed at. I try to preclude this by prefacing the question with a simple statement; for example, "Many people experience ghosts" or "Many people see ghosts." This seems to offer enough openness on my part to let the client know that I am sympathetic to his or her world view. A problem with which I have wrestled is how much I should reinforce such beliefs, especially in clients who feel that ghosts have some sort of power or control over them. My basic sense is that I need to empower such clients to reverse this situation without making a futile attempt to alter their world view. This is delicate work, which must be saved for mid-phase, when trust levels have increased and the client's resistances and defenses are better known to the counselor.

Clients should be asked about the presence of a spirit house in their home or on their property, and also at their place of work. A basic tenet of the "ghostology" of Thailand is that restless spirits of the dead tend to disturb people but can be placated by providing them with spirit houses to live in and occasional sticks of incense or gifts of food. Although I have yet to do so, I would not consider myself above suggesting that a client purchase a spirit house should a ghost be particularly troublesome.

Temple events cover a range of experiences. Most Thai males spend some time as monks in a Buddhist temple in order to earn merit (graces) for their mother. The monkhood is a temporary state for varying periods of time. Whether a male has been a monk or not, and what experiences he has had during that period, are often fertile areas of exploration. Other temple events include the burning of bodies, witnessing the results of natural disasters (the monks are usually part of the relief or clean-up efforts), and contact with astrologers and fortune tellers.

Astrologers and fortune tellers warrant separate mention though. It is not uncommon to have important decisions made only after consulting an astrologer or fortune teller (for example, a palm reader). The counselor new to Thailand will be surprised to discover that no major construction is undertaken unless the astrologers are consulted, the spirits on the site placated, and the spirits in the adjacent areas accounted for and considered. It remains commonplace to leave a corner of a major downtown construction site vacant for the placement of a spirit house. This may be million dollar property where a twenty-five story international bank building is going up! I mention this to emphasize that we, as counselors, cannot take these areas lightly; our Thai clients take them very seriously. The metaphysical is an important dimension of the Thai world view. The counselor who wants to take this world view seriously will have to expend a considerable amount of time questioning and reflecting. It is very important that each counselor be acutely aware of his or her own feelings and biases related to paranormal or liminal events. The counselor who conveys a sense of disbelief or who discounts such experiences will have little success in counseling Thais, and indeed in counseling most peoples of the Third World.

Most Westerners have heard of the concept of karma in Buddhist religion. While realizing that I cannot do justice to the Buddhist teachings about karma in a chapter, I will simply say that karma means that good deeds will be rewarded and bad deeds punished, in this life or the next. What goes around comes around. This extends our Western concept of cause and effect considerably. In dealing with sexual behavior and AIDS, I have constantly had to consider issues related to karma. More than one person has told me that whether or not one contracts the AIDS virus is more related to good and bad karma than to sexual behavior. To establish a client's karma belief system is important. Only then can the counselor feel that some sort of mutual starting point has been gained, so that insight into behavior (cause and effect) may begin. A word of warning here: Thai Buddhism is a very syncretistic religion, having incorporated elements of animistic relations, Chinese religions, and Hinduism. A counselor should not feel that simply reading about karma will be enough. Each client must be queried as to his or her specific beliefs. This would also apply to other aspects of Buddhism. The reading would supply a good background, but it should be considered just that, a background.

I consider myself to be quite eclectic in my therapeutic approach and have found this to be very helpful here in Thailand. But an area which is difficult is the exploration of feelings. To again drastically simplify Buddhist teaching, I will quote my friend Mr. Gasemo, who said, "The goal is not to be a plus or a minus, but a zero." This means that, for Buddhists, feelings are to be subdued, whether they are feelings of sadness or joy. This is the "middle way." On the other hand, and this is where the puzzle begins for me, the Thai language has a marvelous array of "feeling words." Sometimes I have had clients who would not articulate their feelings, and I felt that this was their reality, that their feelings were so well suppressed that they operated at that ideal zero level. In such a case I may ask the client to "imagine how it might have felt," or I may just shift out of the feeling mode to "What were you thinking at the time?" On other occasions I have felt that clients were afraid to admit their feelings to me because this would indicate that they had not achieved the zero level. This I could interpret as a defense, as posturing. But even when feelings are expressed, the language barrier comes into play. Most of the feeling words do not have direct translations. Feelings is a tough area, and I find myself processing this frequently.

Pastoral counseling across cultures is a great challenge. Of the many ministries I have performed overseas, I can honestly say that no other has lead me to such serious considerations of language and culture as the engagement of a local person in a counseling process. In this process it is vitally important that I clarify my understanding of a client in culture, language, and nuance. It has also been imperative that I look closely at my own beliefs and world view. Attentiveness to counter transferences is so important—and the pursuant discovery that we are sometimes angry with aspects of culture that we do not understand. A byproduct of attempting to counsel others has been an increased understanding of the other Westerners who are trying to inculturate themselves and learn how to cope. Having worked through the feelings that have arisen in myself as a result of "bumping into" another culture, I feel more competent in assisting others here in Thailand as they try to do the same.

The considerations of the Thai world view that I have mentioned in this chapter are some of the important considerations I have learned to bring to each Thai client. There are many others that arise from single episodes, or from special circumstances (for example, children of second or third wives). The basic tenets I employ here fall back on something I learned early in my career as a pastoral counselor: I never assume, and I never pretend. I make it my goal to model honestly for a client any "differentness" through being open about cultural or personal qualities I do not understand. I find that the client's attempts at clarification help both of us. I find that it also helps clients to be honest with the areas of their personality or world view which are unclear to them as well. Some of the best counseling work I have done across cultures has happened when at mid-phase a client and I both admit that we are completely puzzled about what is going on. Then our exploration together takes on a new honesty, and counseling becomes a mutual effort. Sometimes, but not often, I even think that I understand what is behind that Thai smile!

8

KOREA

THADDEUS CHANG-SOK KIM

Father Thaddeus Kim has been focusing on the integration of the Eastern way of psychotherapy with the theory and techniques of Western psychotherapy. In particular, he sees major points of convergence between Eastern Tao and the Western existential/transpersonal psychotherapy.

For example, they share the goals of peak mental health and the highest maturity. In addition, both Eastern Tao and Western existential therapy rely heavily on a unique spiritual bond between therapist and client, in which therapist participates in the world of the client and the client shares in the enlightenment of the therapist.

As a Pastoral Counselor, I consider myself to be God's chopsticks. In me, as a person, and in my counseling ministry in Korea, the integration of one chopstick (Oriental tradition) with another chopstick (Western psychotherapy) is most imperative.

Since I returned to Korea after completing my studies of pastoral counseling at Loyola, the first difficulty I encountered was the integration of Western psychotherapy and Eastern mentality. Not only in theories that I studied in the classrooms but also in actual counseling sessions with clients I find a sort of discrepancy or struggle in me between what I studied in the school and what has been embedded in me through an intricate web of various cultural influences. Dongshick Rhee, a Korean psychiatrist, claims that Western psychotherapy started in the twentieth century whereas Eastern Tao started twenty-five hundred years ago.

I understand that many Western psychotherapists are increasingly becoming interested in Eastern Tao (literally, "Way" or mysticism). In 1928

C. G. Jung received from Richard Wilhelm a Chinese writing called *The Secret of the Golden Flower.* This was the first time the Western world became interested in Taoism in relation to psychotherapy and counseling. In the 1930s Karen Horney, Erich Fromm, and many other psychotherapists, counselors, and clinical psychologists became interested in Tao, and particularly in Zen Buddhism. Erich Fromm wrote *Psychoanalysis and Zen Buddhism.* Karen Horney went to Japan to study Zen. R. D. Laing was in India for two years for Taoist training in mysticism. According to *On Becoming a Person* (Rogers 1961), Carl Rogers was in China in 1922, and his philosophy of interpersonal relationships was influenced by his stay there. F. Perls studied Zen in Japan and wrote a book called *In and Out of the Garbage Pail* (Perls 1972).

However, their understanding of Eastern Tao has not been satisfactory. Some understand it as a derivative of magic, some as regression in the service of the ego, some as the total experience, and so on. Allan Watts and Fingerette seem to have had a fairly comprehensive understanding. The former called Eastern religions different ways of psychotherapy in the Western sense. The latter considered that the results and the crucial psychological progresses of both the Western psychotherapy and the Eastern mysticism are the same. Kelman suggests that vaster and deeper possibilities are open in the direction of the Eastern Tao master/disciple relationship. Max Hammer, an American professor of psychology, wrote a book called *Quiet Mind Therapy*, in which he emphasized the Oriental way of meditation and mysticism. Medard Boss, a colleague of Martin Heidegger, maintains that in terms of purification of mind, the best Western psychoanalytic training is only an introductory course. In the 1960s Anthony J. Sutich developed the idea of transcendental psychology from the philosophy of Tao. The so-called third-world psychology appeared as humanistic and existential psychologies, characterized by trans-personal psychology, which can be called Taoistic psychology, in essence.

On the other hand, many Eastern (Asian) psychiatrists and psychotherapists insist that the Western psychotherapy or theory and the principle of psychoanalysis are not easily applicable to Asian clients. The reasons probably are that Asians are reluctant in expressing their feelings, and their family system is utterly authoritarian. And yet, they either have little understanding of Eastern Tao or reject it. The purpose of my entire study at Loyola was to clarify the confusion (in me) that existed between the Eastern way of psychotherapy and the Western psychotherapy and also possibly existential thought by showing the common elements among them.

GOALS OF TAO AND WESTERN PSYCHOTHERAPY

In Buddhism the goal of practicing Tao is to become a Buddha (a saint or an angel) by liberating oneself from attachment (bondage) and reaching emptiness (non-attachment).

In Confucianism one becomes a sage by liberating oneself from desire and reaching the stage of no-desire (the Mean). In Lao-tzu's teaching one becomes a true man by liberating oneself from striving and thereby reaching the stage of doing nothing (Wu-wei). In Chuang-tzu's teaching one becomes a peak man (a perfect man) by liberating oneself from the sufferings of birth and death, thereby reaching the state of being freed from being hung upside down. In psychoanalysis one becomes one's own real self by being freed from one's major instinctive motivations of the id, or neurotic feelings. In humanistic person-centered psychology one becomes self-actualized by freeing oneself from deficiency motivations. In transpersonal psychology one transcends the self.

Attachments, desire, striving, sufferings of birth and death, major instinctive motivations of the id, and deficiency motivations are different names for the same thing, that is, mental illnesses and defects. Emptiness, the Mean, doing nothing, being freed from being hung upside down, the real self, and self-actualization are also different names for the same thing, that is, peak mental health or the highest maturity. Both Rogerian and Buddhist approaches consider the causes of psychological problems as alienation of the self from reality.

PROCEDURES AND PROCESS

Psychoanalysis asks the person being analyzed to verbalize, without hesitation, everything that comes to mind. The Tao practice demands the disciple to observe whatever comes up in mind and body and make the disciple aware of his or her ownership of it. Rogers's study of the process of psychotherapy reveals that clients express their negative feelings first when asked to report frankly what occurred in their mind. For instance, when "John" begins to disclose his hidden feelings, he says his mother is the most loving person in the world. Then he may say, "I seem to have some bad feelings toward my mother." When this negative feeling comes to the peak, his mother becomes his worst enemy. After he exhausts his negative feelings toward his mother, others, and the world, he can feel and express positive feelings toward them. Then his mother becomes the loving person again.

This process can be compared with the 360 degree transformation in the Zen practice. When one starts the Zen practice, one starts at the zero degree point. Here one's mother is the most loving person. In the Zen practice "mountain is mountain and water is water." When one starts to observe one's inner world, one feels negative feelings about self, others, and the world which had been repressed and caused neurotic symptoms. The point at which one pours out all the negative feelings is the 180 degree point at which "mountain is not mountain and water is not water anymore." This is a complete reversal of values and perception. Here one's mother becomes the worst enemy in the world. If one exhausts all the negative feelings, then one feels positive feelings only. When one exhausts all the positive feelings, then one returns to the original point: "Mother is not your enemy but a loving one again; mountain is mountain and water is water again." These are not the old distorted or one-sided images, but they are completely revealed, genuine, real beings. This is the total acceptance and understanding without one's own projection. Now one has returned to the original zero degree point but has traveled 360 degrees. This is the state of subject/object congruence. Reality has always both positive and negative aspects at the same time (Yin and Yang, Darkness and Light). When one starts at the zero point, one's negative feelings are repressed, and one's positive feelings are also repressed. After the 360 degrees excursion one moves to the genuine, true, undistorted, complete picture of oneself without projection. This is what we call the original face of oneself: Buddha, true man, sage, peak man, or "Juchaesong" (self-identity), which can be reached after complete purification of mind.

Ta-Hui, one of the Zen masters, says in his *Letters* that when one has a conflict, he should think or express any kind of emotion and try to find the origins of the thoughts and emotions until he exhausts these to the bottom, and then one is one's original, genuine self. He also says that one is enlightened (Nirvana), when one has already removed "something stuck in the chest" (conflict or stress). Further, he says that when one is enlightened (Nirvana), one's dreams and reality become congruent; in psychoanalysis, dreams are related to reality. In the Zen circles people say you have to kill your father and mother, even the Buddha, in order to be enlightened (Nirvana). This is quite similar to being freed from authority or the resolution of the Oedipal conflict.

A paragraph from Lao-tzu's *Tao Te Ching* is frequently quoted in Zen literatures: "The student learns by daily increment. Tao (Way or enlightenment) is gained by daily losses—loss upon loss until it comes to Wu-wei (doing nothing)." This means that when you study a theory or concept, your knowledge increases every day. But when you practice Tao, you lose your neurotic motivation until you gradually lose it completely. This is the meaning of doing nothing (Wu-wei). Wu-wei is the complete loss of any neurotic desire or motivation. I believe R. D. Laing understood the meaning of Wu-wei well when he said that a real Taoist person can cure patients by his mere presence doing nothing (Wu-wei).

THE THERAPIST AND BODHISATTVA

In psychoanalysis, to be able to analyze others one has to be analyzed successfully by another analyst. In Zen Buddhism, likewise, one has to be enlightened, awakened to self, in order to be able to help others to be enlightened. There are four ways to help others. One is giving material things or money. Next come loving words. The third way is doing beneficial deeds. The fourth and best way is "doing things together." (It is noteworthy to compare this idea with the spirit of community in the Christian tradition.) When Bodhisattva helps a thief, he becomes a thief himself. This is the ultimate form of a therapist's participating in the client's world. In the humanistic, existential approach the therapist does not consider the client as someone different from the therapist himself or herself. In *The Great Awakening of Faith*, a Chinese classic, it is described that a Bodhisattva does not consider the non-enlightened (Jungsaeng) as different from himself. And a Bodhisattva does not think he is helping. This means that therapists should not think that they are superior to the client, and that they are giving help from a higher position. The Bodhisattva's personhood, therefore, is very important. R. D. Laing, Hans Strupp, and many others emphasized the importance of the therapist's personality, claiming that even the same techniques bear different results depending on different types of persons, that is to say, that the results of psychotherapy depend on the personality of the therapist, not what kinds of techniques are used. Jung seemed to have this in mind when he said, quoting a Chinese axiom, that if a therapist is bad, the result of the therapy will also be bad, no matter how good the therapeutic techniques used.

DIFFERENCES IN BELIEF SYSTEMS

A brief review of literatures highlights the significant differences in belief systems among the various religious perspectives. Christianity and Judaism are monotheistic, but Christianity's trinitarian doctrine departs from Judaism. Zen Buddhism and existentialism share an emphasis upon spontaneity, immediacy, and clarity of awareness, and are open to insights from diverse traditions of thought and therapy. Paul Tillich tried to meet God, a supreme being. Atheistic existentialism accepts the concept of non-being. In atheistic existentialism, however, one meets "self," just as in Taoism, which can solve the problem of existential anxiety. Although some religious beliefs are discrete, such as Christianity and Judaism, the philosophical insights of existentialism and Zen are sometimes shared even by adherents to Jewish and Christian faiths. It is interesting to note that Fromm claimed the image of God in human beings (according to Christianity) to be similar to the idea of Buddha (according to Buddhism). However, the Zen doctrine of enlightenment is by no means shared by all existentialists. Also, Zen does not rely upon belief in any deity, whereas existentialism has theistic and atheistic forms. Shamanism tends to be syncretistic; it borrows from and merges with whatever religions prevail in its cultural environment. Shamanism can be theistic, but it also recognizes the importance of human ancestral and non-human spirits.

Despite these underlying differences, all of these belief systems have common concerns regarding motivations and strategies for human service.

Given the common value commitment to compassionate and moral relationships, each perspective approaches the helping relationship as an "I-thou" relationship. Moreover, each perspective is holistic and ecological in that it addresses the connectedness of the biopsychosocial and spiritual needs of clients. Each perspective utilizes various techniques of prayer, meditation, and ritual to assist clients. It is to be noted that meditation training including Yoga and deep breathing practices is common among Oriental religions, particularly in Zen; these techniques are applied to help clients reduce stress and to enhance self-awareness, concentration, and empathy.

TESTING OF THE RESULTS OF TRAINING AND PSYCHOTHERAPY

Bojo described the method of testing the results of the Zen practice. When one has the objects of love and hate of the past in front of one's face and does not feel love and hate, one's Tao is ripened. Even though one's Tao is ripened, one is still not free of love and hate. When one meets the objects of love and hate and is made to feel love and hate, if one still does not feel love and hate, one is completely liberated. The third patriarch of China Seng-tsan said in *Inscribed on the Believing Mind* (Hsin-Hsin-Ming), "Only when freed from love and hate, one reveals oneself fully and without disguise." This corresponds to the fact that the central features of every psychoanalytic treatment are love (dependency) and hate (hostility) toward the analyst.

LEARNING AND REALITY

In Eastern thought one always distinguishes between Tao (reality) and teaching (learning or theory). In the doctrine of the Mean (Chung Yung), "What heaven has conferred is called *nature*; an accordance with this Nature is called *Tao*; the practice of Tao (training for accordance with Nature) is called *instruction*." Scriptural teachings (sutras) are only the dead words of Buddha and only the means for attaining the Buddha-mind. In Zen Buddhism, Buddha-mind or Reality is called the *moon* and the scriptural teaching (theory) the *finger pointing at the moon*. After you see the moon by the help of the pointing finger, you should forget the finger (the theory or instruction). It teaches, "Leave the words. And cut the thoughts. Get the meaning and forget the words. Then you become friendly with Tao."

There are three profound gates to prevent the diseases of the Zen practice that interfere with entering enlightenment. The first gate is to understand the highest scriptural teachings (theory); the second is to forget this theoretical or conceptual understanding and focus on "here and now" (reality perception) through Zen dialogue (Koan); the third and the most profound is to cut the words which remain, by silence for a while, or by complete silence, or by striking with a stick, shouting, striking the Zen table, and so on. It is quite natural that the third gate is the most profound, since the essence of Sakyamuni's discovery consisted in the realization that every kind of physical and mental torturing is of no use and that cutting the outside appearance and illuminating one's own mind are the only solution. The third gate forces the disciple to realize this. The best theory or technique is nothing but the description of the mind or the conduct of the most mature or the most purified.

COMPARATIVE REMARKS

I have so far described some important similarities of the Eastern Tao and Western psychotherapy and the existential approach. Eastern Tao emphasizes the positive, the reality, self-training, becoming Bodhisattva. Western psychotherapy seems to be more theory-technique oriented and tends to be more verbal. The existential and humanistic approaches seem to be closer to the Eastern approach. Dongshick Rhee, a Korean psychotherapist, claims that in Western psychotherapy and the existential or humanistic philosophy one can remove neurotic anxiety but not existential anxiety, whereas in Eastern Tao one aims to remove this existential anxiety, which originates from the fear of death, by facing death without fear. Tao transcends the personal experience and culture and becomes congruent with the ultimate reality. Western existential and humanistic thinking is in a sense the gate that leads to Eastern Tao. Tao tries to solve the awareness of the fear of death. Transpersonal psychotherapy also tries to do just that.

It seems important to note the difference between the two great religions of the East, Confucianism and Taoism, which started about 2,000 B.C. in China. Confucianism held its place in morals, while Taoism reigned supreme as the effective system of relating the worlds of mystery and humanity. Taoism made capital out of Oriental quietism and proposed passive mystical accord with heaven as the highest goal. Confucianism stressed the deed and proposed that human conducts regulate themselves in active harmony with heaven. Thus, it is impossible to separate Taoism and Confucianism. Unlike Western religions, they are not an organized, systematic influence on people, but rather are inherent in the Korean culture.

Western psychotherapy emphasizes the resolution of emotional conflicts, while Eastern psychotherapy is interested in transcending the conflicts. Therefore, introduction of Western psychotherapy into Korea should not be considered as transplanting something alien into the Korean culture but rather as grafting procedures onto an already existing philosophical and goal-directed model of emotional care.

The traditional Korean personality and culture, which foster a tightly knit family structure and warm interactional relations, make the existential and humanistic psychotherapy highly suitable to Koreans. Although it is generally accepted in Korea that withholding emotional feelings is a virtue and expressing them a weakness, it is becoming commonplace for many Koreans to express their feelings and even verbalize anger. This trend might pave the way for better verbalization of feelings to psychotherapists who have studied Western psychologies.

It is amazing to note that Oriental philosophies are being studied in the West more than in the Orient. But there are some Oriental students of psychology who are beginning to be interested in Oriental philosophies. Both Westerners and Easterners should seek the integration of Western and Oriental philosophies of psychology, that is science and Tao. Thus, two chopsticks (Eastern Tao and Western psychotherapy) can be united to serve humankind better in every corner of the earth.

AUSTRALIA
&
EUROPE

9

AUSTRALIA

THOMAS KEARNEY

Brother Thomas Kearney, a member of the Irish Christian Brothers, under-took studies in pastoral counseling after twenty years as a teacher and school principal in the state of Victoria in Australia. Upon returning to his homeland, he became pastoral counselor and coordinator of campus min-istry at the Australian Catholic University in Ballarat, Victoria.

Brother Kearney found that he had a new role in campus ministry as he attempted to facilitate change and to promote growth in both individuals and in the campus community as a whole. Kearney's pastoral perspective permeates his reflections, finding in the work a challenge to his own growth.

In reflecting on the ongoing need for pastoral counseling, Brother Kear-ney writes: "I have a sense that there will always be a role for the pastoral counselor in the many and varied ministries in our church and our world. Whenever there are people who are not free, who are in pain, there will be a need for others to bring to them the knowledge that Jesus has redeemed them, that there is the possibility for them to be free and to respond to the call and the hope of their God, that they will have life and have it abun-dantly."

"I want to be my own person," she anxiously demanded. Such was Mar-ia's greeting, as she entered my office. Unannounced, she dramatically broke in on our meeting to plan Thursday's lunchtime liturgy, a most inop-portune time. Fortunately, I was able to usher her into a second room, placate her for the moment, get back to the liturgy group, bring its meeting to some conclusion, and return to Maria to work with her in her crisis.

Maria's incursion came early in my life as counselor/campus minister at the Ballarat Campus of Australian Catholic University. Part of her confusion came from a phobia of being in front of others, part from the confusion of her own identity as the daughter of an immigrant from Croatia with all its implications, and part from her desire to be like other Australians.

BACKGROUND OF A UNIQUE COUNTRY

Australia is a young country, not yet a century old as a nation. Barely two hundred years have passed since Europeans settled in the great South land. The first settlement was the establishment of a British penal colony in 1788. The original inhabitants, both the convicts and the free settlers, came mostly from England, Ireland, and Scotland. When gold was discovered in the 1850s there was a rush of people from all over, but again mostly European, a few from China, and some from the gold fields of California.

Self government and later federation established a migration policy, labeled "White Australia," that protected an identity as a European oasis in the southeast Pacific. This was consolidated with a strong tie with Britain as the mother country.

After World War II there was a shift in direction with a move toward the United States. The alliance established as a result of the war in the Pacific led to a strong influence of American culture on the formation of Australian people. We became exposed to Coca-Cola and Pepsi, to rock and roll, to the explosion in American film and television, and to the multinational corporations.

Australia is a large country, in area the size of the United States of America, in population just seventeen million people. These people are predominantly of European descent, but as a result of relatively recent immigration initiatives and the abandonment of the "White Australia" policy, Asian people are beginning to move into the bigger cities.

Our two biggest cities, Sydney (four million) and Melbourne (three million), are both spread over a great area and most of the people live in the great suburban sprawls that surround these cosmopolitan cities. The various population groups have their particular networks, with the Asian groups particularly obvious in their districts. The various waves of migrant peoples have managed to live side by side with a minimum of disturbance. The spread of the suburbs has ensured that people, by and large, have family space to live in comfortably. Outside the major cities the mix of population groups is less obvious.

The strong sense of "the government provides" has continued from the time of the original convict settlement. This has given the country a sense of a welfare system with government funding, at least partially, of education, community health, and a system of benefits for the less fortunate, for example, the elderly, incapacitated, and unemployed. A strong sense of social justice has developed among the people in some ways, but it has also been at the cost of a gentleness in the people. The "Gallipoli toughness" of the First World War Australians came from battling the British and the natural elements in setting up the original country communities. The battle to survive in a vast country bred a group of individualistic people, who handed on a tradition of being hard to their sons and daughters. That was part of the legacy.

Another part of the legacy was the strong feeling that new people "can make a go of it" in Australia. There is the possibility of a new start, which holds a fascination for many people who come to Australia for this very purpose.

Aquinas Campus is situated in Ballarat, a provincial city of eighty thousand people, some sixty miles northwest of Melbourne. The population of the area is overwhelmingly of Anglo-Saxon descent. The Mediterranean and Asian people who have migrated to Melbourne have not yet spread to this region in significant numbers. The surrounding area is rural and supports a mixed agricultural industry of potato growing, and sheep and dairy farming. Because Aquinas is the only rural campus of Australian Catholic University, it draws students from the country areas of the Eastern states of Australia.

THE AIMS AND OPPORTUNITIES OF CAMPUS MINISTRY

In *Creative Ministry* Henri Nouwen refers to Ministry as "the ongoing attempt to put one's own search for God, with all the moments of pain and joy, despair and hope, at the disposal of those who want to join this search but do not know how" (Nouwen 1971, 116). To put one's own search for God and the meaning of life at the disposal of others carries risk. Yet this risk is at the foundation of the work. Australian young people carry the history of a country of hard-working, individualist forebears into a world that is vastly different from that of their ancestors. That kind of tradition is now less relevant than before and no longer suits a people who have no choice but to belong to the "global village" of the whole world.

The appointment as counselor and coordinator of campus ministry, which required a pastoral counseling role and an outreach role, set the context of the ministry with which I was entrusted. It brought a variety of daily demands, which certainly stretched my personal resources.

Campus ministry is a rather broad field and encompasses service to all members of a particular campus. In our case the campus is a rather small group, about seven hundred full time students who are primarily in the 18-25 age group. Most of these students come to Ballarat from distances as great as thousands of miles. It has a supportive role to the main focus of the lives of the students, their study.

In summarizing the skills of the campus minister, Nouwen (1969) states that the campus minister should offer a *climate* in which the student can raise basic questions without fear, a *word* which is an honest response to individual needs, and a *home* where intimacy can be experienced with a vital balance between closeness and distance. At Aquinas this has meant challenging the students to go beyond the comfortable existence that living in rural Australia has provided and assisting them in becoming independent of the strong family ties.

Essentially, campus ministry has as its purpose to encourage and support the members of the campus to gain maximum personal and spiritual development from the opportunities provided on the campus. So, the people of campus ministry attempt to develop and offer to the students opportunities to animate and integrate the various aspects of their personal growth with a spiritual dimension. Campus ministry provides some opportunities for further reflection on what is happening, chances to ponder the important place in their lives of the gospel and spiritual values they encounter on the campus. In this way they will be empowered to meet the challenges of new problems in a changing world and be able to engage in responsible social action.

Campus ministry aims to facilitate change and to promote growth in individuals and in the campus community. It is about *faith* development, about *personal* development, and about *community* development.

Worship is an important part of the faith development of the community. Opportunities are provided for members of the community to become involved in the planning and in the celebration of Eucharist on the campus. In this way we can become a worshiping community. Members are offered the possibilities of assuming leadership roles in the celebration, through the various eucharistic ministries. A liturgy group coordinates the celebration and makes an effort to ensure that the celebration is relevant to the needs of the members. We encourage students to be involved in such a group, because it is a great opportunity to develop one's faith life. Courses are also offered for the training of members to undertake these ministries, (for example lectors, special ministers of the Eucharist, leaders of music) in a more enlightened and meaningful way.

Reflection on what is happening in the daily concerns of life is an important contribution to making sense and meaning of our lives. Periods of time are offered to all campus members to participate in this fruitful exercise. A "Reflection on Life" day is offered to each member of the campus as part of the normal program. This is a chance to get away from the familiar surroundings in order to pray and reflect on the relationship to our God and where we fit into the world God has made. Further opportunities for those who wish to deepen their faith life are advertised through campus bulletins and notice boards.

Praying alone, and finding time to do so, is often a difficult challenge. Praying with a group can be a means of support for individuals. Hence, we promote this opportunity. Interested people are put in contact with the groups that already exist or assistance is provided to those who wish to set up such a group with particular needs.

Each person on the campus is encouraged to be the best person he or she can be. We in campus ministry exist to support each in this personal development. We have become the first stop for any of the students facing problems—from financial, or housing, or study progress problems to personal problems. We also offer counseling as a service through the Centre. In this area we have been able to assist students in clarifying options, and encouraging and empowering them to take greater control over their own lives. We have been able to assist them in growing as people through their personal relationships, their changed living situations, or coming to terms with their own feelings and emotional states. We have been able to help them in the process of understanding and developing further strategies to cope with the immediate situation they find themselves in.

As part of community development the Campus Ministry Centre organizes an Orientation Camp at the commencement of the college year and promotes a Peer Support Program in an effort to integrate the new students into the community. This has been developed to meet the needs of the new students in settling in to the city, in establishing the routines that will be helpful in living a balanced life in the "new lifestyle," especially for those who are living away from home and family, living in shared accommodation, or getting used to being independent for the first time.

The Centre also assists the Student Representative Council (SRC) in its endeavors to enliven the spirit of the campus. Through the activities of its various committees, the SRC provides many opportunities for the students to enrich their own lives and to bring a sense of belonging among the members. Volunteer work is also arranged through groups such as St. Vincent de Paul or in an Inter-Church Cafe, developed as a drop-in center for young people in the city.

The university provides an education with a thrust based on the values of the Catholic church. Hence it brings to its programs, courses, and services an approach built around respect for the individual person and his or her place in the world created by God. The importance of the person is foremost in the minds of the people associated with campus ministry, especially recognizing the individual's journey through life in faithful response to the call of God.

The cultural setting in which I am currently working is a world of young people, university students, mostly full time. It is a world of people, full of potential, who are generally orientated to a life of service. A large proportion is enrolled in nursing and teaching courses, with hopes of working in religious-based hospitals and schools. It has much in common with the setting of all campus ministry work. The needs of Australian students are similar to those of all university students in first-world countries.

MY PERSONAL BACKGROUND AND GOALS FOR MINISTRY

The pastoral counselor approaches people with a sense of the wonder of God's mystery in creation. I can still hear Barry Estadt, of Loyola College in Maryland, enthusing that each person is an individual revelation of God and brings a proclamation of God's presence. The perspective I take to campus ministry work, especially to counseling, comes from my own notions of God, of person, and the relationship between God and people.

My own early family experience was lived in an environment where God and church were fairly important. I was taught prayers, taken to church regularly, and encouraged to participate in church services and events, including youth group. I was educated in Catholic primary and secondary schools. There was a consistency in my experience that seemed to confirm that there was more to life than just what was happening around me in this world. There was more to living than having things, even being comfortable with the people around me, parents and friends. All this is consistent with being a third generation Australian of Irish descent. The Irish heritage was a strong influence in Australia, especially in the Catholic church.

What my faith was saying to me was that my God was calling me, and all of us, to a life beyond this, a life with God. This life in some ways was a "learning to be" so that we could be with God. Somehow, God was important and interested in me. I could have a relationship with God that meant something to me and my completion as a person. This belief, and this relationship, helped me make some sense of my life as I journeyed through many experiences.

This background led me to ponder a life of service in ministry. I encountered a group of men, the Congregation of (Irish) Christian Brothers, imbued with the spirit of their founder, Edmund Rice. In 1802 Rice had responded to a call to serve God in the education of the poor boys of Waterford, Ireland. Now these men, dedicated in consecrated brotherhood to bringing the gospel to youth within the mission of the church, touched my life. Through their work in schools and in the care of youth they challenged me to bring such a fraternal dimension to my relationship to others based on my belief in this loving God.

I believe that my God is actively revealing himself to me through scripture, through my life experience, through my attempts to pray and relate to him, through my experiences of church and other people. The call to me and to all people is to go beyond the here and now: "The Kingdom of God is within you" (Luke 17:21).

The message contained in John 10:10, "I have come that you may have life, and have it in abundance," is part of the hope that God has for all of us. This comes through the free acceptance by Jesus of the role of Redeemer. Jesus, too, by his life showed us the way to the Father. We too can make our claim on a loving God.

The Spirit-Lifegiver continues to be present in our world, through the church, the Kingdom people, to give the life we need. The life of the Kingdom continues through the response we make to the call of Jesus to be with him and his people through ministry.

I believe that I am called to participate in this work Jesus began, to work and serve that people may have life and have it in its fullness. It is an invitation to bring the values of the gospel to all aspects of my living and dealing with others. In essence, it is a call to work from a basic respect for each person and for the growth of each at his or her own rate. I am to proclaim the gospel, to affirm the dignity of each person, and to work for peace in a just society. Such is the challenge of ministry.

As I think about my own view of human nature, I see that people, created in the image of God, have a spiritual side to their lives that enables them to know and choose freely. This free will means that each is free to respond to God without being forced to. I need to acknowledge the different cultural heritage of each student as this shapes the way each responds freely to this call through life.

The book of Genesis tells of the fall, that human nature is flawed by sin, resulting in a struggle to reclaim the intended perfection, to make our own the redemption won by Christ. The struggle has the element of overcoming physical and spiritual impairment in one's life, as well as in the lives of other people in our social group. The challenge of life is for us to integrate the various stages of growth as we voyage. We are fortunate that we can be helped by our fellow travelers and a Christ who has been across the waters before us.

I recall two ideas the Director of Pastoral Counseling at Loyola College, Mel Blanchette, raised with us in class. First, each person has the right to be free. This is a part of our birthright that can be easily lost through the influence of other people, or through allowing our inner feelings to get out of balance. Second, each of us needs to deal with the pain caused by the tension between expectation and existence, the wish and the reality. This is particularly the case with the recently arrived migrants and their children.

When I move into a counseling session I assume that the pastoral counselor serves by being with, by bringing acceptance of, the person in the process of responding to a difficult stage in the voyage of life. I have to understand the process of integration, the various dimensions of the problem being faced, and the pain and loneliness of decision-making. I need to appreciate, too, how freeing it is to divest oneself of a problem and to be able to enjoy life more fully and more responsibly.

THE PASTORAL COUNSELOR IN AUSTRALIA

To be a pastoral counselor in Australia is to work on the fringe of most people's world. There is no easily recognized role for such a person. In fact, it is often associated with our pastoral industry and farmers. Neither the role of counselor nor the perspective of being pastoral are well understood and accepted in Australia. The endeavor is breaking new ground.

Why has counseling taken so long to develop in a country such as Australia? I believe it has something to do with the independence that is so highly valued. Australians do not wear their hearts on their sleeves, nor do they like to admit that they cannot sort out their own problems This is particularly true of the men.

The concept of counselor on the university campus has been more related to career guidance and course selection than to personal counseling. The latter has been a recent development and one that still needs some selling to the student body.

The concept of counseling—especially in a formal way—is not one familiar to the community at large. It has still to win acceptance from the general population. The role of the professional counselor or the mental-health professional is a growing one as the speed of life, and its pressures, become more evident. In a provincial city such as Ballarat there are only six entries in the local telephone book under psychologists/counselors and six agencies (three associated with church groups).

Most counseling experienced by Australians has been of an informal nature. It has taken place through contact with a local church person, or perhaps the local general medical practitioner. It would be the "abnormal" person who would be seeing a counselor on a regular basis. Hence, there is still a fear of the counseling process in the minds of most people. It is very much an unknown. There are no advertised pastoral counselors in private practice in Ballarat, or probably in most cities in Australia. There are very few pastoral counselors, as distinct from clergy (men or women), practicing in the parishes of the land. Some formal structure is beginning to come with the establishment of agencies such as Centrecare, Catholic Family Services, and Uniting Church Outreach. But it is far from the formal structures that are prevalent in the United States. There is not yet a pressure from the general population for such a service; however, recent trends in family and community life are beginning to create the need.

OVERCOMING INITIAL RELUCTANCE TO COUNSELING

The number of students who come for personal counseling is relatively few (approximately 2 percent). It is good to have them evaluate the experience as positive. "It is good to have people to go to for a chat," they say. It is thought of as an informal arrangement, especially good for others, but, for most, "I do not need it." To even come near a counselor is a big step for an Australian.

My experience in campus ministry seems to have verified this. For the first few months of my work, there was very little call on me for counseling work. My work load was mostly in developing programs for the liturgy group and its needs, in supporting the work of the St. Vincent de Paul Conference and its initiatives, and in helping to develop the work of the Peer Support Program. Fortunately, for the first semester I was also doing some teaching work. These contacts with the student body, although only with small groups within the body, enabled other students to assess the worth of the new counselor. This was also happening with those who approached for the less threatening hassles such as applying for student loans, seeking assistance in applying for government assistance, and in seeking assistance for housing arrangements about the town.

Availability to attend to the needs of the students was the strongest way of building up their trust. After some time acceptance gradually grew. It showed itself in the greetings and the sharing of some of the news of the social life of the campus.

In my initial meeting with students I make a special effort to attend to the needs that are most apparent, not to rush into a full diagnosis. This listening and the respect paid to the story told and to the student have been the critical ingredients in the early stages of relationship. The foundations are then established for the possibility of future work. Certainly nothing will be achieved if this is not present.

The warmth of the relationship not only establishes some credibility, but is also part of the therapeutic value of pastoral counseling. The client needs to experience the acceptance and the possibility of the love of God acting in their lives. This is difficult for the "normal" Australian to accept, having been inculcated in the model of the tough, independent person never in need of help. Counseling brings the chance of reconciliation and a liberation from the inhibitions that bind the clients. This creates the context in which the pain of the client can be addressed, the person in sorrow can be comforted, and the burdens can be shared.

EXAMPLES OF PASTORAL COUNSELING IN CAMPUS MINISTRY

I first met Maria when she came to me to discuss her continuation as a nursing student. She was having great difficulty giving tutorials in front of her peers. Whenever she had to give a tutorial she would have a panic attack, often to the point of being violently ill. She faced great difficulty in doing examinations. She felt that she was on trial.

As Maria presented her problem, I was faced with the task of helping her clarify the issue of her continuing as a student, which depended on her being able to complete the necessary tasks associated with the courses she had undertaken. She would also need to address another problem; that is, what was behind the tension she felt whenever she had to be out in front, or felt she was being looked at or assessed by others. The expectations of parents who had come to Australia to make a new start and expected her to achieve at the highest level seemed to be playing on her mind.

The more Maria told her story, the more I was convinced that she was suffering from a phobia, possibly social phobia. Upon further discussion I discovered that she had been in contact with a psychologist downtown. I was able to encourage her to continue to work with the psychologist in addressing the problem of the phobia. For my part, I needed to work with her about her decision to continue study. This required that I go through the process with her of clarifying the options and consequences, and be with her in the decision. When she decided to suspend study, apply for leave of absence for a semester, I was able to help her with the letter to the course coordinator and to be with her as advocate when the course committee considered her application. She then took advantage of my being available most days to come and "sound off." Eventually Maria gave me permission to speak with the psychologist about my concerns. This enabled me to encourage her in her work with the psychologist and to continue to remind her that she needed to trust her psychologist and gradually address the causes of the phobia and to develop ways of dealing with the fears.

Most of the counseling work I become involved with is reasonably short term. It has been connected with various crises that students tend to meet in their lives.

Sonia, a girl of part Aboriginal descent, had great anxiety about the way she was performing in assignment work. So we worked for a few sessions on expectations, pressures to succeed, effort expended on study, study methods, and some time management. Part of the difficulty was the pressure she placed on herself, believing she was carrying the expectations of her people. After four visits, Sonia was more confident and at ease with the study part of her life. She is typical of quite a number of students who have sought some counseling.

Evelyn came because she needed to tell someone her grandfather had died and needed to cry for a while. She also needed to clear her mind to work out what to do next, who to tell, how to arrange transport to get home, how to apply for leave and other details.

Sandra's case was different. I had to find her and tell her that her brother had been in a car accident and might either die or be permanently paralyzed. To be with her at the time was difficult. It was not known to me before that her father had been in a similar accident five years before and was away on a rehabilitation program to learn again how to walk. Amid her tears she told me of feeling again the despair she felt when her father's accident occurred. She could not understand why. Neither could I. Again, I was able to help in arranging her next moves—going home, telling lecturers of her absence for the next few days, arranging to tell some of her friends around campus.

Leanne came because she had failed a course for the second time and was asked to show cause why her course should not be terminated. She came to seek help in appealing the decision. When we sat down to talk about the events that led up to the situation, it became evident to her that she was being treated justly, and that, if she had been the supervisor, she would have failed herself. Talking further, she was able to identify a number of issues she wanted to address (her poor self esteem, her lack of confidence, her lack of a sense of direction, poor relationship with parents, lack of independence, and so on). She agreed to meet weekly with me, even though she formally severed her connection with the University.

John, a student in the Diploma of Teaching (Primary) course, was referred to me because he was having great difficulty on his teaching practice. When he came to me he was angry about the treatment he had been given by his supervising teacher and by the supervisor from the university faculty. In working with John over about six or seven sessions, I was able to help him develop a more realistic appreciation of his own self-assessment, of the criteria used in assessment, and then in his own personal approach to life. Some of his problems were associated with partying with friends and not giving attention to the necessary details of preparing work, which led to problems with his supervisors. His drinking habits, too, were fraught with danger and were contributing to his poor performance in class.

For these young people the problems appeared as unique crises. However, they bore many similarities to the crises facing young people whom I had met while studying in Baltimore. The pressures placed on them—by family (functional and dysfunctional), by study, by the expectation of material possessions, mobility, and wealth—are beginning to become very evident in the Australian society. The downturn in the economy, the increase in youth unemployment, and the complications of a multi-cultural society have contributed to a general confusion for the students I meet.

Not surprisingly the counseling cases I was involved with were with young people dealing with self-identity, with separation from parents and family, with establishing themselves in relationship to the world and the people about them. They needed to find the balance among so many differing forces, tensions or pressures in their lives.

The study of personality development has certainly provided a good map to assist me in helping the students find their way through the normal crises that life presents. Knowing that their experiences are "normal" is very helpful to most of them. It is just that we go through the crises in our own distinctive ways. Given the nature of the counseling position and the nature of the clientele, young university students, it is not a surprise that the caseload is filled with short-term, crisis-oriented clients. Their problems are not uniquely Australian, but rather the crises of young people growing up in a world becoming more success oriented, more materialistic in its expectations, and increasingly less family orientated. They need help to find their way in such a world.

THE ROLE OF THE PASTORAL COUNSELOR

As I ponder the role of the pastoral counselor, I am reminded of the metaphor of a ship sailing the seas of life.

As an Australian, having lived on an island continent for all of my life, I have some familiarity with the seas. It seems an ideal image, as one does make a journey through life, traversing the seas under varying conditions, some favorable, some less so. The challenges in mastering the waters are akin to the challenges one faces in mastering the experience of living as separate, yet interdependent people in this world.

The role of the counselor can be seen as one ship traversing the seas, accompanying others. If I am to be brother, which I am called to be by my vocation, and fellow sailing ship for others, then it will be in being with others and accepting them as they evaluate their journeys, in understanding what is happening on the journey and, if necessary, in helping them change direction.

The courses studied at Loyola exposed me to the theories of people such as Erikson, Levinson, Freud, Jung, Adler, May, Glasser, and the theories of the family therapists such as Minuchin, Haley, and their associates. These have helped me to bring some understanding to what is happening for others. The contact with the work of people such as Carl Rogers reminds me of the importance of the relationship between the counselor and the client. The "unconditional positive regard" that Rogers talks of brings a power of its own.

My acceptance of Leanne, John, and Sonia gave them the respect that they needed and empowered them to take the necessary steps to change their lives, to set new directions for their journeys. My acceptance of their worth as growing people encouraged them to take responsibility for maximizing their self-awareness and growth, to challenge any faulty foundational premises or goals, and to renew their efforts to change their behavior.

I see my role as that of one who accepts and respects my clients and helps them to bring about the changes they want to bring about. This may mean helping them to identify faulty thinking, damaging behavior, and frightful consequences. This may mean helping them to develop a healthy way of thinking, of behaving, and of planning for a better outcome from the effort they are making.

In this way I can see myself being able to ride the seas in the company of others, assisting them to evaluate the waves and the breezes of the life process, and if necessary, to make corrections so that they can finish the course at the place they had hoped for and not get caught up in the wild winds of the open seas and be blown off course.

After all, if I am to be the ship that bears the precious cargo, it is Jesus who is the sailor, the helmsman on the trip. It is from him that the directions and the course setting are gained.

THE COUNSELOR'S CALL TO BE "BROTHER"

Working with these young people as they struggle to make some sense of what has been going on for them has been an enriching experience. I have come to appreciate the sacredness of each of their journeys. My office has been a sacred space for the time that we have worked together in it.

More and more I have come to understand the concepts of the developmental psychologists — that we progress through many stages as we journey through life. Each of us is special in our own separate way. We come to explore the various experiences, and as we integrate them into our lives we come to make sense of them. It is part of our growing and, as Robert Kegan (1982) says, life is about making meaning and keeping the competing interests in our life in some form of balance.

Working with Sonia helped me to realize that we all expend energy in particular ways that, sometimes, do not get us the results we hope for. We gradually come to understand our limits and begin to be able to work within those limits. I was able to work with her to apply her skills in study in a more realistic way. There was a great sense of personal satisfaction when Sonia announced that she was much more comfortable about the pressures of her study life and felt she could now handle her situation much better.

Being with Maria in her pain was rather uncomfortable. I felt in a bind for professional reasons. I needed constantly to remind myself that she was under the care of another counselor. My encouragement to her to trust the other and to continue attending counseling sessions was the best I could do. At the same time I felt that it was necessary for her to have a place where she could leave some of her concerns about what was happening to her when the anxiety attacks occurred. It was less uncomfortable when she gave me permission to contact her psychologist. Then I was able to report my observations and place at the disposal of another counselor some insights that Maria had not yet spoken to her about. These helped to fill out the picture.

The experience of working with Maria reminded me of something our clinical supervisor had mentioned to us frequently — the necessity of a team approach to case management and the professional responsibility that we have as counselors to make sure that the clients are the focus, not our own satisfaction or need to be in control of the decision-making.

The experience of working with John helped me to appreciate more the role of the counselor to walk beside and to help explore what is going on. John needed to share his anger at the perceived injustice he had suffered at the hands of the supervisors. I felt for him as he told his version of the experience. Part of this involved his teaching religious education lessons on the images of God to a grade six class and an alleged lack of preparation. Part of this, too, was related to his own perception of God. Between his faith development problems and the burning desire to be accepted by his peers, there was much for John to journey through. Sharing his story was certainly a sacred experience for me. It also put me in touch with my own journey in faith, and I began to reflect on the compassion, forgiveness, and understanding of our God. I was inspired that John was in there struggling to come to terms with this challenge to his faith and where his relationship with God was leading him. How could one be other than inspired by such courage? I was able to be for John part of the healing touch of a God who loved him. In this case "to brother" certainly meant to walk beside and be with, for I could not offer him a simple answer that would solve all the problems. It was something tied up with experience—that on a human level and on a supernatural level there would be an acceptance of him and his struggle, and that it was all right.

So, I have found that there is a real challenge to my own growth as I try to understand what is going on for others—for Sonia, John, Maria, and for Leanne, with whom I am currently still involved. To be empathetic and compassionate and to respond to the challenge is of itself a growth-producing exercise. It has been also a faith-developing experience. I have been able to experience some of the challenge of meeting the suffering Jesus in my brothers and sisters. If I am able to be with them, to offer the drink of water, then I am ministering to the Lord himself, and being true to my call to be brother.

THE EXPERIENCE FOR THE STUDENT

Most of the students who come with the minor problems are very much relieved to think that someone can listen to them and develop with them some options they can try. Their immediate concerns are that they have run out of options and do not know where to go next. This is very helpful whether the concern is a matter of a financial difficulty, or a concern with lecturers, study progress or of appeals against what they consider some injustice. To have someone listen is a great starting point and an affirmation of them as people.

To have a caring listener is also very valuable when the problems are a bit more complicated. It was helpful for Maria to talk to someone who did not dismiss her concerns lightly, who understood what she was talking about. The more comfortable she became, because of the positive reception she received, the more she was able to understand what was happening to her by the way she spoke about her past experiences. This allowed me to encourage her in the progress she was making with her psychologist downtown. Hopefully, this will contribute to helping her develop her power to manage her life more successfully.

John's experience seemed to be that he, too, was empowered to make significant changes in his way of life through our work together. Through investigating with him some of the consequences of his actions, he was able to better assess his own talents and gifts. This gave him a better base from which to launch his teaching preparation. His understanding of his faith also grew as we explored what was in the gospels and in the church and in his experience. He felt much more comfortable about talking about his God and his own growing in faith. He did not need to have all the answers, and maybe he never would have all the answers, but his understanding of what he believed was changing, was growing, was developing, and that was good. He began also to take more control over what he did, especially his drinking. So, for him, the counseling experience was positive, and he recognized this.

For Leanne the early stages of the counseling relationship have been painful. It has not been easy for her to get in touch with what is happening for her. To be under the microscope is difficult. Wanting to change, and having the capacity and the insight necessary to bring about this change, are two separate things. Leanne is finding this out. Not being a student anymore, and not getting a job easily, and being on unemployment benefits can be elements leading to despair. At the funeral of a friend, who had recently died of leukemia, she wondered why it could not have been her rather than her friend who had died. This is proving to be a challenging position for both of us. My experience with the others is an encouragement as Leanne and I progress through some stormy seas together.

Despite the painful and difficult stages that have been part of the counseling experience for these clients, counseling has been a positive growing experience for each of them. It further promotes the concept of the power of "presence" for people. To be present for them and with them has great healing power. I trust that I shall always remember this in my dealings with the students I encounter in the role as counselor in campus ministry.

THE NATURE OF PASTORAL COUNSELING

The process of pastoral counseling is similar in many ways to that of general psychological counseling. In both cases clients share a personal story that helps them establish contact with the foundations of their own life.

The focus of general counseling is the lifestyle of the client. Its health and fundamental values are examined in an atmosphere of objectivity, warmth, and acceptance. The counselor may need to challenge, to confront, the values or the underlying cognitive processes, which may be the source of the lack of growth or the failure to deal with the tasks of life.

I believe that people become who they are through the learning process, through the interaction of what they have inherited with the environment in which they live. Most of our problems as humans are comprised of components—thoughts, feelings, and actions, including interactions with others. Resolution of these problems can require some direct intervention. Counseling could be described as corrective learning.

The process of counseling can be described in stages. It requires the establishment of a positive relationship between the counselor and the client. It needs some functional analysis, some diagnosis, a statement of what change is desired. Then a rationale, an explanation of the scenario is established. The client needs to know what is happening. The counselor needs to initiate some kind of restructuring, explaining, of the behavior and to set up some form of corrective learning. This approach to counseling requires the active participation of both the counselor and the client in bringing about the change sought by the client. What, then, is pastoral counseling?

Are all counselors pastoral? James E. Sullivan makes the following points:

> All counselors are pastoral in the sense that all are concerned for the suffering, the depressed and confused. However, the pastoral counselor approaches his work from a framework and a value system that is God-oriented. He does not force his value system on his clients but his particular value system gives him (1) a greater sense of the dignity of the person as a child of God, a brother (or sister) in Christ as well as (2) a greater motivation to reach the client with the redeeming love of Christ. In a word the *what* of all counseling is pastoral. Perhaps also the *how*. It is the *why*—the personal framework value system and motivation of the pastoral counselors that makes pastoral counseling different from other counseling (cited in Estadt 1983, 20).

The nature of pastoral counseling is found in the dimension of the relationship, and in the motivation of the counselor. It is here that the model for the relationship is dramatized in the scriptures for us in the image of Jesus as the Good Shepherd. There is a dimension of personal individual concern for the hurt and lost sheep—so much so that the ninety-nine safe sheep are left in the care of each other and the lost sheep is actively sought out and saved from the marauding predators. The Good Shepherd models the presence that the pastoral counselor must exhibit toward the client. The attitude of respect, which has been mentioned above, toward the client is the primary source of the healing and reconciliation that the pastoral counselor can bring.

TOWARD A THEORY OF COUNSELING

Each of us brings to counseling our experience and our knowledge. In essence, we develop a theory of counseling from the knowledge base and from working with the various clients we meet.

I have come from the experience of growing up in a Catholic family, from the experience of twenty-six years of religious life as a Christian Brother, and from the experience of being a high school teacher for just over twenty years. This journey through life so far has been important in establishing some foundational values about people and the way they could live their lives.

I have come to understand that each of us is a unique person, with a particular body (determined by genes and chromosomes) and spirit (which provides us with the capacity to know and love, to make choices based on this knowledge, experience, and desire). However, we do have a need as humans to share life with one another. By nature we are relational beings. Part of our fulfillment is in relating to others—love, intimacy, communication, and social behavior are important parts of our living. As we live in family and society, people (parents, peers, teachers) and social institutions have significant influence on the substance of our growth and experience, and on how we grow through that contact.

My own experience has left me with a notion that people are, by and large, good, and they choose their own patterns of behavior. The values that each person operates by are acquired from the parents, peers, school, church, and community that they interact with. Socially acceptable behavior brings approval, and unacceptable behavior some disapproval.

We do choose our own path in life through our response to what goes on around us. The knowledge I acquired at Loyola helped me to create a way of understanding my experience. The psychology taught gave me a way of looking at my experience from the intra-personal dynamics as well as the interpersonal dynamics. It gave possible explanations for the various experiences through the theories we were exposed to. This also gives me the possibility of understanding and explaining to others what may be happening for them.

All this has been a contribution to my formulating a theory of counseling, but I am not sure yet that there *is* any one theory of pastoral counseling.

My work at Aquinas in campus ministry has strengthened my belief in the value of being present for the other. This seems to be very true for the young adults I am working with. This has given them the power to make some significant changes in their own lives. It is a source of encouragement and empowerment. To know that someone is on their side helps them continue when the going gets tough.

THE FUTURE OF PASTORAL COUNSELING IN AUSTRALIA

What lies ahead is unknown,
a source of mystery and apprehension.
Perhaps the allure of the sailing life
—always moving, always changing,
always wondering what the next passage will be like,
and what we will discover at the other end.

Captain Armin. E. Elsaesser III wrote these words in the log book of the "Pride of Baltimore" on May 7, 1986, just before the Pride met her end in Chesapeake Bay. These words speak of the uncertainty of the future, yet also of the mystery that the future holds for us.

Pastoral counseling seems to me to have some part in this future. In

Australia, and especially in campus ministry in Australia, there is a role for the pastoral counselor. Given the pressures that seem to build up for us in the hasty way we try to live our lives, it appears that there will be an even greater need for the pastoral counselor to help us to stay in touch with ourselves. It is ever so easy for us to lose our way. We need to find supportive people in our lives to be with us as we traverse the seas of life.

I am beginning to understand the importance of such a role in the work I am currently involved with, that of campus ministry at university level. To be with young people as they encounter some of life's difficulties and to help them find their way is very rewarding personally. To assist others in understanding some of what is happening for them and what they are experiencing is to introduce them to a sense of self-worth. I suspect from the experience of my own voyage, I may be able to offer an acceptance and an openness to the possibilities that are around for others. My patience and presence may be an assurance as they navigate the difficult waters of such times.

I have a sense that there will always be a role for the pastoral counselor in many and varied ministries in our churches and our world. Wherever there are people who are not free, who are in pain, there will be a need for others to bring to them the knowledge that Jesus has redeemed them, that there is the possibility for them to be free and to respond to the call and the hope of their God, and that they can have life and have it abundantly.

This role will be different from that of the pastoral counselors in United States. In Australia their work will be more informal, certainly in the immediate future. It will be a supportive role for people as they come to discover the spiritual dimension of life. It will probably develop from the outreach work of the various Christian churches. The changing pressures of the secular world will lead people to seek the caring people from the Christian world.

10

THE NETHERLANDS

HENDRIKUS VERBAKEL

Father Hendrikus Verbakel of the Netherlands, nearing completion of doctoral studies in pastoral counseling, reflects on the status of the field within his country. Beginning with an overview of major sociological changes, he outlines their impact on the expectations of the churches, noting that clergy find themselves inadequately prepared among a wide array of highly educated mental health practitioners. While an increasing number of clergy involved in hospitals, penitentiaries, universities, and military services have had opportunities for developing counseling skills, very few would identify themselves as pastoral counselors.

As Father Verbakel looks to future developments in the field of pastoral care and counseling, he calls for further ministry preparation in psychology and helping skills and more extensive networking among clergy and members of the secular helping professions.

Whoever enters the Netherlands on a clear day by air, and lands at Amsterdam airport, will have an indelible impression of land divided into small rectangular units segmented by a myriad of canals and ditches. Looking from above and observing from a distance, the idea is instilled that this small country consists of numerous little islands separated by water and connected again by bridges. It looks as if this small, crowded country consists of people, who each live on their own little site and form in their gestalt a complicated labyrinth. This impression will be strengthened by a visit to cities such as Amsterdam and Delft, with their numerous canals and bridges. It appears as if water is everywhere, and the Dutch have been solely occupied with the building of bridges in order to escape the natural island features of their landscape.

141

However, this hasty first impression is more than just a tourist view of a country. I would like to present this image as a metaphor indicative for many features of the Dutch culture, the place of religion and church within this culture, for example, as well as the position of pastoral counseling.

HISTORICAL REMARKS

In order to gain an understanding with regard to the mental health situation in the Netherlands, it is necessary to address briefly its history. This overview will be condensed to basic notions only; it lacks every pretention of being comprehensive. Some remarks will be made from a sociological frame of reference, some observations will be made from a religious point of view, and finally the secular field of mental health will be addressed.

SOCIOLOGICAL OBSERVATIONS

Up until well into the 1950s Dutch society was strongly determined by compartmentalization of its citizens. Each major social, political, and especially religious participant in society had its own structure, in which every segment of life was organized. Education, (mental) health care, politics, unions, but also activities such as sports and dancing were organized according to this segregated principle. To be a Roman Catholic, for example, entailed not only an expression of religious belief and commitment, but participation in a series of well-defined, organizational structures. In sum, each religious organization or quasi-religious organization became a self-sustained "island." These bigger or smaller "islands" served a series of purposes. The "island" concept protected the identity of the group, organized plausibility structures for its members, functioned as a defense mechanism against everything what was considered alien and potentially harmful for the group, and—especially in the case of the Catholic community—served as a major tool for social and political emancipation. It was the success of this strategy that led to a relative equilibrium of political, social, and economic power.

However, success was also the beginning of disintegration. Again, primarily referring to the Roman Catholic segment of Dutch society, several features of this process can be distinguished. The spirit of the Second Vatican Council, the increased longing to democratize society, and newly acquired self-esteem among many members started an eroding process of this labyrinth of well-known compartments of society (Thurlings 1978; 1979). Bridges were built, and people started to move from their "island." This process resulted in rapid secularization, decreased participation in church life, and eventually a new quest for identity of each composed segment.

The breadth of these changes came clearly to the surface in a sociological study in the early 1980s. Felling, Peters, and Schreuder concluded that the core of the Dutch national identity was no longer formed by traditional religion. They observed this trend away from a Christian view at the world, especially among young people and those who were well-educated. They concluded as well that a traditional religious frame of reference was replaced, in part, by a new emphasis on moralism (Felling, Peters, and Schreuder 1982).

OBSERVATIONS WITH REGARD TO RELIGION

It is not difficult to understand that within this frame of reference the changes for church life and especially for ministers and priests have been considerable. Although church and political society were firmly separated, within the monolithic group, the role, identity, and competence of religious personnel were stable and well-defined. Outside of the "island," the priest or minister might have the features of a clown, a fake, or at the very best a representative of a competitive structure, but inside the "island" his role was ipso facto justified. Secularization and the outward movement fragmented this position; it shifted the challenges from maintenance of the institution and its sociological "fall out" toward development of new paradigms of pastoral care.

Heitink identifies a series of these recent developments within the realm of pastoral care in the Netherlands. The priest/minister finds himself among a wide array of mental health practitioners. These practitioners are highly educated and trained in a specific area of expertise. This development questions the priest/minister's credentials in the field of the helping relationships and urges a higher degree of professionalism. Concomitant with this quest for professionalism, Heitink identifies the need for specialism, which he defines as "expertise in a specific sector." Leaders of religious communities face a new and challenging set of demands due to social differentiation and diversification. Clergy are also asked to perform professionally in a wide array of fields: hospitals, army, penitentiaries, hospices, and so on — the sectors of life that need specific pastoral capacities and expertise.

Heitink also points at another trend in contemporary pastoral care, which coincides with the above described sociological shifts: the emphasis on individual pastoral care. Whereas several decades ago church activities were largely determined by maintenance of the organizational structure, the eroding process caused both liberation and confusion for the individual in his and her quest for meaning and direction in life. In both instances the individual is in need of a new formulation of faith and understanding of self, somewhat separate from the church's encompassing notions.

It is, beyond any doubt, these shifts in pastoral care that urged a new (or renewed) frame of reference and required additional expertise and competence of religious personnel (Heitink 1991). Before addressing the impact of these dissimilar processes for pastoral care in general, and pastoral counseling in particular, some brief remarks need to be made about mental health practice in the Netherlands.

OBSERVATIONS WITH REGARD TO MENTAL HEALTH PRACTITIONERS

It will cause no amazement that in the highly compartmentalized Dutch society, mental health practice developed along similar segmented lines. Initially the intramural health care like hospitals and psychiatric wards, initiated by various church denominations, were closely linked with their founders. Being admitted to a Catholic hospital meant literally to be exposed to an entire arrangement of Catholic customs and rituals, safe-guarded by priests and nuns. Religion had its "natural" predominant place, and the importance and necessity of those who represented the organiza-tion was unquestioned. Due to the sociological shifts described above, the decline in religious personnel, and last but not least, the growing control of the government, which became the sole financial supporter of these institutions, the influence of religion and church life became increasingly peripheral. Where institutions presently classify themselves "Catholic" or "Protestant," the label signifies hardly a firm identity; many of these insti-tutions are recently trying to come to terms with the meaning of this clas-sification for their services to the general public. In many instances the religious inheritance has been dropped, and neutral institutions have evolved.

Concomitant with these developments, the field of secular counseling and psychotherapy in the Netherlands has increasingly widened and broad-ened since World War II. Dijkstra and Van Donselaar divide the history of psychotherapy in the Netherlands into the following stages. Since the beginning of this century up until 1945, a modest start focused predomi-nantly on psychoanalytic psychotherapy. After the Second World War there was a growing expansion of the psychotherapeutic practice, which eventu-ally mushroomed in the 1960s and 1970s. It was in this era that the major, subsidized, regional outpatient mental health facilities (the so-called "Riagg's"), and psychological and psychiatric societies were established. Dijkstra and Van Donselaar observe in recent years a relative decline in the use of psychotherapy (Dijkstra and Van Donselaar 1988).

PRESENT CONDITIONS

If and how are these developments in society and church life faced? What initiatives are taken by the churches' leadership and clergy persons alike to meet the new demands? And what is the status quo of the secular field of mental health professionals? How — if at all — are religious questions and spirituality in general practice addressed? This section will attempt to give insight into the manner Dutchmen try to respond to these develop-ments.

RELIGIOUS FIELD

The signaled identity crises with regard to clergy persons in the Netherlands, due to rapidly changing socio-cultural structures, have been counteracted by a series of changes and adjustments. In the formation of future clergy persons a greater emphasis has been placed on the scientific study of these socio-cultural changes by a further strengthening of disciplines such as sociology, psychology, and pastoral theology. At the same time pastoral field education with its array of supervision and intervision has gained significant prominence. Additional course work and supervision has also been implemented for ministers and priests. These developments started in the middle of the 1960s and have progressed ever since.

These major changes in formation and education of prospective clergy persons would have been impossible without the introduction of Clinical Pastoral Education (CPE) in the Netherlands. CPE was started in the early 1960s by Zijlstra, who received his training as supervisor at the Menninger Foundation in Topeka (USA). This introduction meant a major shift in theological reflection and ministerial training. For the first time a systematic approach was adopted for inductive theology, and an educational road was paved for "learning by doing." The parishioner/patient/client became systematically the focus of pastoral care and counseling, and subject rather than object of the proclamation of God's word. The word *systemic* refers to a theoretical context, based on theological and psychological considerations, and translated into an educational curriculum; it is, of course, irrational to state that before the introduction of CPE no inductive theological reflection and/or learning by doing had been practiced.

As in the United States, the introduction of CPE in the Netherlands became immensely popular and has definitely changed the lives of numerous priests and ministers. Its introduction also increased the interest in psychology and psychotherapeutic theories and strategies and changed the manner in which pastoral care was conducted. Another side effect was an increased interest—certainly during the late 1960s and early 1970s—in multi-disciplinary collaboration between clergy persons and other health practitioners. This last development decreased, however, in the last decade, due to the growing shortage of ministers and subsequent increase of work pressure, the impact of continued secularization, and a lack of clear strategy for these encounters between religious personnel and other health practitioners.

The emphasis on CPE-training in the Netherlands enhanced as well the integration of personal and spiritual facets of life, in combination with a growing professional outlook within the clergy persons. Many of the clergy persons who concluded the intense three-month training and decided to continue with their profession described their experiences as fundamental, and instrumental for facing the challenges at later stages of career and life (see Firet, Berger, Vossen 1991).

On a theoretical level, the CPE-training is, among others, supported by the study meetings and publications of the Catholic Study Center for Mental Health (Katholiek Studiecentrum voor Geestelijk Gezondheid = KSGV). This center has been active for more than sixty years and plays a significant role in the dialogue among psychology, theology, and pastoral care in the Dutch church, an influence substantially bigger than the Roman Catholic community alone.

SECULAR FIELD

With regard to the developments within the secular mental health profession, the following remarks need to be made. First of all, many professional organizations for mental health workers in the Netherlands have been established since the beginning of the 1960s. Congruent with American developments, the mental health field, in reaction to a strict psychoanalytic perspective, started to divide into different theoretical orientations. This trend coincided with growth in interest and use of psychotherapy. At this moment, seventeen professional organizations are officially registered, among which the Dutch Institute for Psychologists (Nederlands Instituut voor Psychologen = NIP) and the Dutch Organization for Psychotherapy (Nederlandse Vereninging voor Psychotherapie = NVP) form the umbrella organizations (see Bel, Jonkergouw 1991).

These organizations have a strict psychotherapeutic character and are in many ways involved in the scientific, professional, and social enhancement of the profession. It is noteworthy to point out that none of these institutions incorporates religion and spirituality as a part of its professional trade; that is, no organizational provisions are at hand for the study and implementation of religious aspects of human life in a psychotherapeutic frame of reference. In other words, religion is neither hindered nor positively reinforced by professionals in mental health. Nonetheless, it would be a mistake to presume that none of the mental health professionals officially listed as psychotherapists is aware of these questions and potentialities. The list of supervisors of the Institute for Rogerian Psychotherapy in 1990, for instance, counts four members with formal theological education among its 154 participants.

It is, of course, impossible to estimate the number of psychotherapists with an active and scientific interest in the religious and spiritual aspects of their clients, beyond diagnostic and psychopathological levels. That this interest is not completely omitted is demonstrated by a thin but steady stream of literature with regard to meaning, values, and religious perspectives within the Dutch psychotherapeutic realm (see Dijkhuis, Mooren 1988; Debats 1988). Instrumental in this regard are the study and research efforts of the Psychology Department of Culture and Religion of the University of Nijmegen. This department is the only center in the country that specializes in scientific psychological study of religion. However, in accordance with van Belzen in his congratulatory article for W. J. Berger at his seventieth birthday, and who headed this department for more than a decade, one might assess that this institute has more influence in the theological realm than it has had in generating significant inroads in the psychological domain (van Belzen 1989, 492).

In sum, the fostering of professional psychotherapeutic study and research, and its implementation into actual treatment, is relatively well-developed in the Netherlands and measures adequately in comparison with international standards. However, in contrast with, for instance, the situation in the United States, religion and spirituality play hardly a visible role within the psychotherapeutic establishment, and hardly any organizational structures are in place to further the study and implementation of religion and spirituality in the psychotherapeutic domain. No organization exists in the Netherlands for pastoral counseling/psychotherapy.

PASTORAL COUNSELING/PSYCHOTHERAPY

In order to conclude this section about the state of affairs of mental health care in the Netherlands, and the place of pastoral counseling/psychotherapy in particular, the following remarks need to be made. I utilize for this purpose the clear, but rather functional — and therefore limited — classification of Browning (see also van der Ven 1991). He divides the field of ministry into three separate categories: pastoral care, pastoral counseling, and pastoral psychotherapy. Pastoral care is the most generic and inclusive of the three; Browning perceives all unstructured and communicative activities between pastor and others (parishioners or not) as manifestations of pastoral care insofar as religious, ethical, and psychological perspectives are held together. Pastoral counseling differs from pastoral care by its structured nature, in which the pastor designates specific time and attention in order to help the individual with his or her problems. Pastoral counseling presupposes an understanding of psychological developmental issues, as well as a moral and religious perspective on human behavior. Pastoral psychotherapy, on the other hand, is a more specialized form of pastoral counseling in which the setting, the structure, and the techniques used are more proficient than those used in pastoral counseling. Consequently, pastoral psychotherapeutic activities resemble the goals of psychotherapy in general. Hence, pastoral psychotherapy assumes an even more elaborate understanding of psychological and developmental issues, but a well-developed comprehension of the Jewish and Christian perspectives remains imperative.

Utilizing this classification, the developments over the last decades in the Netherlands can be assessed as follows. The introduction of CPE, the changes in formation and training of religious personnel, and the increasing emphasis on supervision and intervision have without doubt changed the content and quality of pastoral care. Whereas clergy persons trained before the sixties had hardly been exposed to human sciences, and pastoral theology in its implementation to direct pastoral care was hardly developed, the changes over the past decades have changed this state of affairs and enabled clergy persons to become more professional and competent in their craftsmanship with a wide array of pastoral activities. With regard to pastoral counseling itself, the situation is hardly developed. It is likely that clergy persons who are employed in hospitals, penitentiaries, universities, and military services will develop extensive pastoral counseling skills, and even fewer will identify themselves as pastoral counselors. In contrast with the situation in the United States, hardly any clergy person will enter the general mental health field as pastoral counselor. Consequently, the dialogue between pastoral counselors and other mental health practitioners is virtually nonexistent.

Aside from a handful of clergy persons with degrees in clinical psychology and mostly employed in "Riagg's," and a few clinical psychologists with an elaborate theological understanding, pastoral psychotherapy is virtually a nonentity in the Netherlands. Pastoral psychotherapy as a separate and distinct discipline among the different groups of mental health practitioners does not exist.

PERSPECTIVES

The landscape of the Netherlands, with its abundant number of rectangular tracts of land divided by ditches and canals, is not solely a tourist attraction, but an image for many facets of the Dutch society. Ministry, and pastoral counseling in particular, share this state of affairs. However, Dutchmen have always been able to build bridges; driven by the necessity to survive the unpredictable nature of existence, and the innate wish to communicate with others, they have had to reach out for what is foreign and unknown.

This final section shares some suggestions and thoughts about the nature of these "bridges" with regard to pastoral counseling and its related areas. Some of these proposals might occur as platitudes for a too complex reality, others might bear the features of Utopian thinking. However, Utopia — understood as the pursuit to build on reality in the hope to reach out for what is behind the horizons of life — is by its nature a Christian act. It takes soil, fertility, seed, a sower, and care for the crop before the promised harvest can be collected, either thirty, sixty or hundredfold.

Bridge #1. In general, the training and education of clergy persons in clinical psychology, psychopathology, psychology of religion, and basic psychotherapeutic techniques need to be fostered and strengthened. The purpose of this additional training is not to turn ministers and priests into psychologists. But those who have responsibility in church life deserve to enhance their capabilities with regard to the total spectrum of pastoral care, detect psychopathological symptoms, and gradually gain a clear understanding of their potentialities and limits with regard to their abilities to help parishioners. This enhancement will facilitate professional ministry, add to the competency of the pastor, and ultimately benefit the well-being of both minister and congregation.

Bridge #2. It will be, for many of the clergy persons, impossible to maintain good and fruitful contacts with a wide array of other mental health practitioners. Nonetheless, it is important that contacts are established and fostered with these different disciplines. The regional coordinators and their staff members, as well as the diocesan service centers, could fill this void and network with pastoral counselors, psychologists, and psychiatrists within the "Riagg's" as well as outside these established organizations.

Bridge #3. Due to the changes in society and pastoral care, and the consequent intensified pressures for clergy persons, the development of platforms for supervision, intervision, and mentorship needs to be increased. Pastoral counselors can play an instrumental role in this growing need within the life of churches.

Bridge #4. In line with Browning, the focus of this article has been exclusively on the role of ordained ministers in pastoral counseling. In sum, this position is centered around the craftsmanship of the clergy person, who after being introduced to social sciences, among which psychology and psychotherapeutic techniques are pivotal, is trained and supervised in the art of pastoral counseling. Ordination and psychotherapeutic training are in this position a sine qua non for pastoral counseling. With regard to the Dutch situation, this position seems outdated for historical reasons and unwarranted for theological reasons. The present status quo of many churches shows an increasing role for lay ministry; certainly within the Catholic church Vatican II has shifted the emphasis. In the Council documents the church is first of all described as the community of priestly people; that is, all members—on the basis of baptism and confirmation— are participants in God's plan of salvation (*Lumen Gentium*, no. 10). There is no apparent reason why lay persons within the churches cannot be educated and trained in the craftsmanship of pastoral counseling. This approach reflects in part an intense discussion within the American Association for Pastoral Counselors (AAPC), which only recently changed its prevailing policies and now allows lay persons with official support of their church leaders to become members.

Bridge #5. An increase in research is imperative for the enhancement of pastoral counseling. This research needs to embrace the cross areas between psychology and theology and focus on the relevance of theological themes for psychotherapeutic/counseling activities. Themes could encompass differing areas such as grace, redemption, sin and guilt, creation, stewardship, symbols, and rites and rituals.

Bridge #6. Although the animosity between churches and religion on the one hand and the psychological world on the other is historically fierce, the time might come soon to start a new dialogue. Both are, at the very least, partners in their different pursuits to further the mental health of human beings and are therefore committed to similar goals. Pastoral counselors need to face the challenge to explain the hindrances and blocks of religion and religious activities, as well as the healing power of religion for the suffering person. This task needs to be done without the indoctrination and desire to snatch the partner with whom the dialogue is initiated in order to produce a convert. It will also show the possibilities and wisdom of the centuries-long tradition of the church community. Perhaps secularization has progressed enough for mental health practitioners and clergy persons alike to bring up the subject again.

EPILOGUE

MARIA RIECKELMAN

Maria Rieckelman MM, MD, has been involved since 1945 in some aspect or other of the healing ministry. Initially as a general medical doctor in Korea and Hong Kong, and later as an adult and child psychiatrist, Maria has pursued avenues of holistic health whether through diagnosis and treatment, education or prevention of illness and disease.

Since 1975, her ministry has been principally to missioners and those who minister to others across cultures in various religious traditions, and in many countries of Asia, Africa, Latin America, as well as North America. Maria gives workshops, retreats, individual therapy and consultation within the spectrum of adult developmental, psychospiritual, and social issues.

At least six months of each year she works in partnership with Fr. John Sullivan, MM, pastoral counselor and spiritual director and from 1977 to 1987 Maria was a member of the Faculty of Loyola's Pastoral Counseling Program.

Good wine-tasting parties are delightful. I feel as though I have just been to one as I complete the varied chapters of *Pastoral Counseling in a Global Church: Voices from the Field.* I sense especially the invigorating freshness of new-made wine, not tasted before and very different from well-aged vintage wines. As I perused the pages of this book I felt as though I tasted dry, heady wines; full-flavored wines; brand new, just developing wines; delicious, almost vintage wines.

Each of us readers has in fact been sipping the fresh new wines of pastoral counseling as it develops in such culturally distant places as Ghana in West Africa and Korea in northern Asia. Indeed, we have tasted the creative blending of pastoral counseling among women and men trained in Loyola's Pastoral Counseling graduate programs. This group of graduates itself, we have discovered, illustrates many pathways of cultural differences.

Thaddeus Kim and Joseph Ghunney, for example, point clearly to these cultural differences.

I believe the most significant feature of this book is its authentically tentative, yet gently rooted nature. Each of its quite different pastoral counselors ventures enthusiastically in pioneer ways to explore areas of difference, mystery, pain, and confusion across cultural, theological, and religious terrain. These differences are both subtle and profound, yet changing almost with each new sunrise.

It is not surprising then that we find ourselves at this juncture of the human story with many questions and untried paths in pastoral counseling across cultures. The questions, the unknowns, the confusion, the struggle evokes in me another image. As I write these reflections, 180,000 people of Homestead, Florida, are doing the initial cleanup after Hurricane Andrew's almost total destruction of their town. In this disaster and out of its rubble, those who have suffered are trying to make sense of their lives, their collapsed homes, their powerlessness. Others—"pastoral ministers"—out of families and friends from many parts of the United States are offering help. Undoubtedly those who are most helpful are those who *listen* well to the *real* basic needs of the disaster victims, to their deep sense of rage, impotence, and loss, to their need for support in genuine friendship.

This reality surfaced by the hurricane provides, I believe, an authentic image for much of the cultural collapse and all-encompassing change that challenges us earth people in the 1990s. We find ourselves at the threshold of this post-modern era with change occurring at lightning speed in almost every major dimension of life—family, culture, religion, theology, self-understanding, gender roles for women and men, work, technology, environment, ecological awareness, communication, politics, geographical boundaries, and the list goes on. Little wonder that pastoral counselors engaging the *other*, of other cultures and religious traditions, find the process so full of awesome questions that have no ready answers. Pastoral counselors themselves are experiencing—to the degree that they are *aware* and *awake*—many radical shifts within themselves, their own values, dreams, behaviors, and so on. And the clients/parishioners/patients seeking assistance are going through their own set of cultural renegotiations. It is as though this great hurricane is swirling around stripping bare the leaves and branches of all our well-rooted plants and trees, all our structures. In the midst of all this disruptive turbulence, the pastoral counselor needs, more than anything, a flexible yet rooted sense of self so as not to be blown away or to become over-defended out of fear or need to be in control of all the answers and new questions.

How are pastoral counselors in the 1990s going to move through the newly forming challenges to a creative future?

Let me suggest some of the basics already alluded to in various chapters of this book. It is interesting to me that chapters 2 and 10 spoke of *bridges*. Geraldine Brake ministers in Panama—the geographical bridge connecting the great continent of South America with Central America via Mexico to North America. Hendrikus Verbakel helps us to understand The Netherlands as he described the important bridges that connect the many watery "living pods" of his homeland. These chapters are the stories and reflections of women and men who are practicing the art and skills of pastoral counseling in places and cultures where pastoral counseling is new.

Cross-cultural pastoral counselors are, I believe, personal "bridges," assisting clients to connect with themselves, their spirit, their reshaping cultural patterns, their faith, and their families and friends. In this age of cultural upheaval they can help clients and groups in their search to discover connections between what is to be retained out of the richness of their own culture and religious traditions, and what needs to be relinquished. Pastoral counselors can be bridges that connect quite simply, provided the counselor is open to newness, wide open to this discovery in his or her own life. A pastoral person *searches, seeks,* and *follows pathways* and does not always need to function by previously set patterns. This is the stuff of *discovery* in pastoral counseling today. Increasingly, pastoral counselors ministering across cultures, often in a multi-cultural setting, will have a precious opportunity to listen *with* their clients and to help rediscover and name their new cultural identity even as it emerges! Pastoral counseling across cultures will offer the opportunity to explore diversity, to heal global insensitivities, to bind wounds of pain born of cultural prejudice, domination, and alienation within and beyond cultures. The individual work with clients *does* lend energy to a whole culture. The education pastoral counselors can do *does* help to heal the divisive wounds of prejudice. The way we choose to minister as this century ends and a new one begins *will* make a difference for the future of our global community.

Clearly, culture taps deeply into the spiritual values of a people. Pastoral counselors intend to integrate these cultural, psychospiritual values into their counseling. Even more, pastoral counselors are most authentic when they help their clients to articulate their personal sources of faith. When God's Spirit breaks through consciously in the emerging counseling process, the client, the culture, and the work of pastoral counseling becomes more whole, and holy.

In each of the chapters of this book the seeds of the above-mentioned skills are evident. Good paradigms of pastoral counseling across cultures will continue to evolve as counselors recognize and search out with their clients of every culture their specialness, their goodness, and their lived response to their own culture.

Further, I believe the best of feminist spiritual perspectives that are changing the lives of women and men around the world are key to personal, communal, and global transformation. These embrace inclusion, empowerment, and partnership.

Inclusion, which invites and explores life-giving differences, helps to create a rich, diverse, and multi-cultural friendship and community.

Empowerment, which enables the client, the pastoral counselor, and the cultural groups to which both belong to become more aware of their creative God-given potential, unleashes energy for life that blesses us all with newness.

Partnership, which authentically draws the client and pastoral counselor into a mutual dialogue and creates avenues of exchange and collaboration, will finally build a strong City of God. That "City" may be within the client, the pastoral counselor, families, communities, and so forth. New kinds of connections with the above characteristics will be the hallmark of a successful, creative pastoral counseling movement across cultures in the twenty-first century. We—all of us—have a lot of new awareness work to do, and I have only hinted at it here. May we all enjoy the journey into discovery of new kinds of listening, new ways of strengthening empowerment, and new depths of experiencing our authentic differences!

Pastoral counselors are helping significantly in weaving the fabric of a new kind of global community as they take leadership in being the "bridge people"—the connecting friends—with peoples of cultures other than their own.

Appendix

PARTNERSHIP PASTORAL COUNSELING

JOHN SULLIVAN

For the past decade, "Ministering to missioners" has been the goal of veteran Maryknoll missioners, Father John Sullivan, pastoral counselor, and Sister Maria Rieckelman, psychiatrist. In this Appendix Father Sullivan reflects on the unique "partnership-ministry" he has shared with Sister Rieckelman in offering workshops to some four thousand missioners in twenty-eight countries of Asia, Africa, and the Americas from 1982 to 1992.

The ministry was born of the desire to accompany missioners as they in turn seek to accompany their brothers and sisters through and beyond the barriers of poverty, language, culture, food, climate, oppression, and violence.

Here, Father Sullivan gives an inspirational and perceptive account of God's Creating Spirit among people becoming community, demonstrating how inclusion and empowerment can move toward a communion of partnership in which solidarity and creativity replace domination and violence.

Chalatenango Cemetery, Providencia Hospital Chapel, University of Central America: these are the names of places newly made holy by the blood of some of the martyrs remembered and revered by the poor—the powerless, the persecuted, the faithful men, women, and children of El Salvador and Central America. In Chalatenango Cemetery rest the bodies of three Maryknoll sisters, two of them murdered, one killed in a flash flood. The chapel is the assassination site of a Salvadoran archbishop. The university is the place of the military massacre of six Jesuit priests and two women coworkers. These women and men are remembered by the "many"—in El Salvador and other countries. They symbolize the tens of thousands of men, women, and children who have given their lives but who are only remembered by "the few," their relatives and loved ones. Their cruel and violent deaths are remembered, but it is their lives, which witnessed to justice, peace, and hope, that continue to give strength to the struggle for the same peace and justice in the Americas, Africa, Asia, and the world. It is among the living, inspired by the dead, that most of today's missioners live and minister.

These were some of my reflections after an unexpected pilgrimage in El Salvador in the spring of 1991. I was there to facilitate a workshop for missioners, to assist them to cope with stress and conflict, to help them speak and live community in the midst of violence. This pilgrimage still inspires me as I write these words, which attempt to describe community formation in places of violence, the encouragement of partnership instead of partisanship, and the promotion of wholeness and health rather than individualism and death. Missioners throughout the world seek to accompany the people of other cultures and churches in their journey of faithfulness to God, creation, and humanity. Most of these people are poor; many are oppressed economically, politically, and militarily. Some of these missioners are chosen to share the fate of the poor.

This appendix is simply a reflection on the missionary experience of partnership in and through pastoral counseling with some of these missioners, specifically over the past ten years (1982-92). A Maryknoll sister and I, each with more than twenty years of mission experience outside the United States, have lived and worked as partners with some four thousand missioners in twenty-eight countries of Asia, Africa, and the Americas through more than twenty workshops and retreats each year. Maria Rieckelman is a sister and psychiatrist, now based in the United States. I, John Sullivan, am a priest and pastoral counselor and am based in Hong Kong. I write these reflections describing the experience of both partners. The missioners are Catholic sisters, priests, brothers, lay associates, and ministers of other Christian denominations. All are English-speaking and principally from the United States, but also from Europe, Latin America, Asia, and Africa. Our model of partnership pastoral counseling has developed over these past ten years and has been consistently valued by the participants. These pages are my attempt to articulate and celebrate this particular experience of partnership-ministry, which seems to rely on the theory and methodology of pastoral counseling while possibly indicating some new dimensions of process and practice.

Partnership is understood and lived much as described by Evelyn and James Whitehead in their book *The Promise of Partnership* (Whitehead and Whitehead 1991). It is a process of communion in which all conscious forms and expressions of domination over—and alienation from—other persons are explicitly rejected. As a partnership team we consistently attempt to model such partnership and to encourage and assist others to do the same. Holistic connections are constantly sought and dualities rejected when recognized. Some of the gatherings are homogeneous in membership; others are quite mixed. Every workshop or retreat, however, seeks to be inclusive and to bring together in community old and young, female and male, friends both married and celibate, Protestant and Catholic, priest, minister, sister, and layperson, host and guest in cultures, through pastoral counseling and spiritual direction.

The pastoral counseling model of relationship, healing, prevention, and creative stimulation has been foundational to these workshops and retreats and their coordination by the partnership team. This model is multi-dimensional. It begins with *invitation,* develops in a *situation,* is focused through *orientation,* and bears fruit by reflection. Each workshop or retreat seeks to be a life process itself, a moving circle, a recreating sphere of interrelating people, experiences, hopes, and creative insights; each seeks to be an experience of community. This life process was once compared to an apple. The red shining skin attracting attention and stimulating initiative is *invitation.* The pulp of the apple is the experience of the participants, past and present, geographical and interrelational. This is the *situation,* which is the "meat" of the process. *Orientation* is provided by the partnership team; the point of reference being God's revealing Spirit within an unfolding framework promoting integration of mind, body, and spirit. *Reflection,* finally, opens this integrating process to the future, to new beginnings. Reflection is like the seeds within the core, within the pulp, within the skin of the apple. These seeds, these reflections, are the beginning of the future.

The participants are missioners; the partner-guides are missioners. All share a common culture, purpose, and commitment to struggle to become one with peoples of other cultures in mind and heart, customs and language. The four-dimensional process promoted by the team helps the missioners become a community themselves, if only for a few days. These missioners are thus empowered by this process and experience to promote the same community experience in their adopted cultures and churches. This process makes community formation possible.

Invitation, situation, orientation, and reflection seem to be the keys to the popularity and value of these workshops and retreats. These four dimensions give body to a creative pastoral counseling model that relies on partnership. The partners go only when and where invited by the possible participants. This invitation includes travel expenses and a mutually agreeable stipend. It is initiated by the participants themselves rather than by any centralized organization. The team goes to the missioners, in their situation and circumstances, rather than vice versa. Orientation is offered and reflection made possible. And this model is working! Composite illustrations from various countries and cultures will help explain why. Specific persons, places, and situations are the basis of these illustrations, but data have been consciously changed and juxtaposed to serve clarity as well as confidentiality.

INVITATION

One of the services offered by the partnership team has been to assist returning and returned missioners in their transition from ministry outside their country of birth to ministry within their local church. Some years ago missionary sisters working in West Africa participated in one of these transition workshops and then began a process of invitation to the partnership team to work with their missioners and other West African co-ministers. This invitation process took place over three years of letters, telephone calls, and visits; it culminated in some ten weeks of workshops in two West African countries. Eleven four-day, live-in workshops were held at various sites with ten to twenty-five participants in each. The local Association of Religious Leaders took care of additional funding for the participants and the team. The workshops were advertised and the 160 participants came by their own choice. They were both local and expatriate sisters, priests, brothers, and seminarians. In these two countries of West Africa, English is the language of formal education. The invitations originally came from expatriate missioners; they in turn invited their local co-ministers, who in turn invited their friends. As the weeks progressed, local ministers became the majority. This was a good example of advertisement by "word of mouth" and of the invitational nature of this whole continuing formation process. The missioners were not sent by any person in authority, nor were any specific reports on groups or individuals expected from the partnership team. The team was invited because of its reputation; the participants were also invited and came with their own specific expectations and strong conscious commitment to work together. They also came with perhaps a less than conscious hope to experience community. The initiative for these workshops was with the participants themselves—they invited, they came, and they worked together. The team helped their initiative bear fruit through content and process. *Invitation* and personal initiative are integral to life-giving pastoral counseling on both individual and group levels.

SITUATION

Workshops and retreats with missioners in Central America illustrate the importance of the situation dimension of this partnership pastoral counseling. *Situation* implies going into the external, geographical space of those extending the invitation and staying with the internalized concerns that fill their inner space. Over the past ten years the team has conducted numerous workshops and retreats in reflection centers and retreat houses in Guatemala, Nicaragua, El Salvador, and Panama. The participants have been in every instance English-speaking missioners. The team goes to the missioners in the cities, towns, and villages where they work. Groups of missioners, usually numbering between ten and twenty, come together in places of choice and convenience to themselves and the team. The place, issues, and content for these gatherings are determined by the participants themselves. These missioners, like other missioners around the world, share many commonalities; they are immersed in the same local situations, culture, and language. They know one another and often live and work with each other. They focus on issues of similar personal and professional identity, relationships with each other and the people, and challenges of the same common local or national situation.

Issues of identity include transition—movement, death, loss, changes in meanings, values and motivation—psychosexual and psychosocial development, ongoing vocational choice, and midlife and aging concerns. Relational concerns cluster around awareness, listening skills and creative communication, interpersonal relationships and community formation, teamwork and partnership, consensus and other decision-making methods. Common challenges of culture, poverty, death and disease, oppression, and violence usually indicate the need and desire of these women and men to reflect more deeply and to discover more creative ways of coping with intrapersonal and interpersonal conflict. They seek ways of living in the midst of cross-cultural stress caused by differences in personalities, language, food, customs, and values. Some live in the midst of systemic violence with no recourse to the external security of government, military, or police, as these pillars of society are often themselves the perpetrators of the violence. Some live with a realistic fear of mutilation and sometimes death, sometimes threatened by word and letter, oftentimes inflicted on local friends and co-workers. The women and men dealing with these issues are people of deep faith in the living God. They are people who have responded to a call to ministry and mission for the reign of God. They are missioners who have freely chosen to accept the invitation to cross over to another culture, usually very different from their own. And they are Christians who have discovered Jesus Christ in their preferential option for the poor by becoming poor and powerless themselves. They look and long for deeper faith, hope, and love. They usually find all three as they come together with one another in trusting, sharing, and reflection. They discover community among themselves, perhaps for the first time.

The following sample highlights the importance of participating in the missioners' situation. Recently the team was invited by an ecumenical support group of a dozen missioners to help them minister in situations of great physical and psychological violence without suffering this violence themselves or becoming violent in their interactions with each other and the people. The government of that country, its military, and police have been notorious for their blatant abuse of human rights in their overreactive efforts to overcome all opposition and remain in power. The country was at that time in the midst of a vicious military stalemate, and violence was the pervading atmosphere of daily existence. Two incidents from the workshop help illustrate the importance of situation in this partnership pastoral counseling model. The first deals with the stresses of the geographical situation itself; the second, with a conflict within the group.

The first incident happened on the way to a quiet retreat house situated in a mountain area full of natural beauty. The group chose this site as a respite from the noise, confusion, and pressures of both living and working areas. However, the retreat house was in an area contested by the government military and the guerillas. A two-hour drive became an eight-hour experience of frustration for the twelve participants and the team. Due to confused communications, the two-vehicle convoy was held up at one military checkpoint for three hours while negotiations for safe passage were conducted, culminating in a further three-hour visit to an armed fortress for detailed registration. Two other members of the group had arrived at the retreat house that morning without incident; they had been responsible for securing passage through the checkpoints for the rest of the group. They waited, wondered, and feared, while the others fussed and fumed. The theme of this workshop was to be "Coping with Violence." The first session began an hour before sunset in a place that had been without electric power since the power lines had been "stolen" some days before. Many felt most of the day had been wasted. The team began with the obvious feelings of the moment. Rage, guilt, fear, and anger were shared by all, including the team. Violence was not a topic but a shared experience. An unexpected and frustrating delay in beginning the workshop became an opportunity to enter more deeply into the reality of the missioners, the people, and their experience of oppression and powerlessness. The actual situation, the site, and the common shared experience brought trust, bonding, and deeper reflection to the group and launched the workshop well.

A second incident highlights the importance of sharing *situation* with a group by being invited into its internal space of relationships, interpersonal dynamics, and conflicts. The members of this support group had been friends and colleagues for a number of years, with considerable awareness and experience of mutual gifts and limitations. In the last hours at the retreat house the participants agreed to do a timed exercise calling for reflection on personal conflicts. Divided into two small groups, they were asked to name and briefly describe personal issues of conflict. They were quickly to decide to discuss only two of these issues, giving the two persons involved a brief but intense experience of inviting assistance and of attentive listening from the other members of each group. One group understood, accepted, and worked very creatively within the guidelines of the exercise. They were able to return on time, ready to share common learnings and enthusiasm with the other group in the brief time left before the close of the workshop. Some of the members of the other group had difficulty hearing and accepting the exercise guidelines. One person's conflict was discussed for the full time; no common learnings were uncovered; frustration was experienced by all due to indirect and negative leadership experienced and allowed by the participants. This group returned late, told the team it was not ready to report, and wanted the rest of the time available to continue its discussion. The team simply asked them to express this need to the other small group, which had been waiting for their return. The group rejected their request. This interaction between the two small groups had not been anticipated but proved to be a deep learning for all concerning the nature of violence and conflict. Members were able to recognize expressions and patterns of violence in themselves, in their interpersonal relationships, their unwillingness to accept and agree on boundaries, their reaction to leadership through passivity and lack of attentiveness. Deep connections were recognized between the violence "out there" and the violent patterns already incorporated and reinforced within themselves. Conflict within the group was acknowledged, and attempts to cope with it by violence were recognized by all. A sense of empowerment grew as passivity and inattentiveness lessened.

ORIENTATION

Orientation is the dimension of this pastoral counseling model in which the partnership team is most active and most in dialogue with the participants. The team helps to create a trusting atmosphere of confidence and confidentiality through personal example and guidelines. It organizes the flow of input and reflection, helping both to unfold gradually and progressively at the group's own pace. The team formulates and refines the reflective exercises and tasks to help the group focus on and learn from experience. It provides and affirms skills for creative personal and group movement that can remain operative after the close of the workshop or retreat. Orientation comes from the Latin word *oriens,* meaning the direction of the rising sun. The team provides this direction, a developmental progression, a pathway to the group, whether through the format of a workshop or of a retreat. It might be useful to write of *orientation* in the context of a typical retreat, and of the final dimension, *reflection* in the context of a workshop. The team provides "guided retreats," in which it lays out themes for each day; these themes flow progressively and build on each other. There are two thirty-minute conferences a day, usually in the morning. Time is provided to the group after the second conference for observations and clarifications. Scriptural suggestions are offered with each conference as well as concise questions for personal reflection during the day. Guideline questions are also offered to assist in the small-group prayerful reflections in which each person is encouraged to participate after supper. These are self-chosen groups of five or six persons who meet for about one hour. Each day begins with reflective prayer leading into the first conference. Silence is usual throughout the day except at supper. The time between conferences in the morning and all afternoon is left free until a shared liturgical celebration just before supper. This time is used for private reflection and also for personal interviews with one member of the partnership team. The team is usually available for five to seven interviews each day. In this way, over the six to eight days of the retreat there is ample time for each participant to have three or more interviews with a member of the team. These interviews are helpful to the participants in their personalization of the daily conferences, clarification and the sorting out of issues, and for spiritual direction and pastoral counseling.

A retreat example from South America might illustrate this service of orientation provided by the team. Twenty-five missioners gathered for a six-day retreat. These sisters, lay missioners, brothers, and priests came together at a retreat house on a Sunday afternoon. An outline of the conference titles and their focus follows:

Sun. eve.	Introductions/Expectations/Settling-in	
Monday	Listening/Awareness Acceptance/Gift of Life	} focus on Self (Identity) }
Tuesday	Friendship/Intimacy, Sexuality/Connectedness	} focus on Others (Intimacy) }
Wednesday	Conflict/Shame Reconciliation	} focus on Community } (Generativity)
Thursday	Community/Ministry Partnership	} }
Friday	Generativity Mission	} focus on Solidarity } with all creation (Integrity)
Sat. A.M.	Integration/Prayer	

A simple developmental approach is evident. Many of the retreats flow along similar lines. Feedback from participants in this retreat spoke of a "safe" atmosphere conducive to self-awareness and acceptance, sharing, listening, reflecting, hoping, and celebrating with peers and partners. Many of these women and men in their experience of community became closer and more trusting friends—with themselves, each other, and God.

REFLECTION

The fourth and final dimension of this partnership pastoral model is *reflection.* A sheet of glass coated with silver, a mirror, reflects the objects placed before it; a sheet of glass on the face of an electronic tube reflects electrical impulses through television. Reflection, as symbolized by both mirror and television, helps to make these workshops and retreats sources of energy and hope for most of the participants. The team tries to mirror this reflection; the participants discover reflection within themselves by experiencing it. The team attempts to model what it encourages, to reflect clearly on the "glass" of its own behavior and interaction—those creative movements of inclusion, empowerment, and lived partnership. A sister-psychiatrist and a priest-counselor work as a team, sharing leadership and responsibility equally. They encourage inclusiveness, "mixed" groups of men and women in various ministries. They respond readily to invitations from such missioners, especially if a common use of the English language makes it possible for ministers of different cultures to come together. They relate to the participants not as students but as peers and co-ministers with them and with each other. They seek more to empower through shared reflection on lived experience than to inform through prepared lectures and the distribution of printed materials. The participants are challenged to be co-ministers to each other, to relate more as partners without domination or alienation, rather than as competitors to be overcome or at least controlled.

The participants are the "experts" in their own lived experience of ministry and mission; the partnership team provides input to help them "mine," dig deeper into, uncover, and discover this experience through personal and group reflection, always in a context of growing mutual trust and shared faith commitment. A frequent observation after a workshop is this: "For the first time, I really valued my own experience and seemed to hear it in a deeper and more challenging way. There was a trusting atmosphere seldom experienced with other missioners; we seemed to learn and grow in hope together; we 'did' community." This is a statement of a second form of reflection, the internalized process itself. The participants, through the guidance and orientation offered by the team, are enabled to uncover more fully their own experience of life and ministry, to discover more deeply their own gifts and limitations, and to recover more enthusiastically their commitment to living, witnessing, and speaking gospel values in life and creative ministry. This twofold reflective process is simple and very demanding of both the team and the participants. It demands honesty and courage to be authentic and useful. For the team, it requires constant dialogue with the participants, beginning with the participants' clear, written expectations during the initial hours of coming together. This is followed by observations from the participants at the end of each day, in which they are invited to state what was helpful and what was not helpful, what was energizing and what was draining, and what movement has taken place toward the fulfillment of the expectations they formulated earlier. Finally, at the end of the workshop, there is a detailed, written evaluation of the content, process, and of the team's and participants' contributions or lack of them. In both workshop and retreat there is time allotted for personal interviews; these conversations also give the team a sense of the group.

The team tries to keep in touch with the group and its movement by meeting alone each morning and evening, and before the sessions in the afternoon when necessary, to share and clarify impressions, to fine-tune and sometimes devise new content for the brief conferences, to formulate and refine the reflective questions and tasks. The team believes that this committed struggle to dialogue promotes creative movement in the group. Their partnership makes such continual listening and response possible. The team members confirm their partnership with each other through their efforts to be in partnership with the group. These moments of dialogue are sometimes difficult but are often the most creative times for all.

In a very real sense the content of these gatherings is the participants themselves; the team helps that content to unfold and be revealed through a reflective process demanding both unstructured quiet time and moments of focused attention and participation. This content is best recorded not in notebooks but in modified attitudes, renewed energy, and fresh commitment. This newness is expressed in a smile and a hope rather than through scribbled words to be filed and forgotten.

An example from a country in Asia portrays this reflective process in the context of a workshop. A religious community of women asked the team to help them finalize a consensus decision on whether or not to remain in that country offering mission ministry. The local church was quite developed, with numerous indigenous sisters, brothers, priests, lay missioners, ministers, and leaders. These sisters had accompanied the local church more than fifty years through great poverty, two wars, and rapid development in every sector of life. Many of the sisters had been in mission in that country for ten to forty years. Below is a description of the daily schedule and process used with this group of women. It is similar to that most frequently used in such live-in workshops.

8:00	Breakfast
9:00	Opening Prayer and Reflection
9:15	Input Session and Guidelines for Private Reflection and Group Exercises
10:00	Private Reflection
10:15	Small-group Reflection, three to six members in each group
11:00	Break
11:15	Small-group Reports and Full-group Observations
11:45	Reflections by the Partnership Team on Reports and Observations
12:30	Lunch and Afternoon Break
3:00	Input Session and Guidelines for Private Reflection and Group Exercises
3:45	Private Reflection
4:00	Small-group Reflection
5:00	Small-group Reports and Full-group Observations

5:30   Reflections by the Partnership Team
6:00   Observations and Evaluation of the Day
6:30   Supper
8:00   Liturgical Celebration

This particular community had been working on its decision to leave or to stay during meetings over the previous eighteen months. The group had consulted extensively with members of the local church. The team had time before and after the workshop for personal interviews with many of the participants. In other workshops, the afternoons often are not so fully scheduled and more time is available for private reflection and personal interviews both in the afternoon and evening. Prayer and liturgical celebration are always part of each day, according to the faith customs and experience of the group. These were days of guided reflection and prayer for this community, and they bore fruit in the sisters' consensus decision and commitment to remain as missioners in that country, but primarily in ministries not yet taken up by local women in ministry.

In summary, invitation, situation, orientation, and reflection certainly seem to be integral to creative pastoral counseling, whether on a one-to-one basis or in the specialized groups described in these pages. Among these missioners, at least, the partnership relationship of the team and the encouragement of partnership as an attitude of life and component of ministry have given challenge and hope to the participants.

Missioners are cross-cultural people, women and men who choose to cross between their culture of birth and their culture of adoption. In their struggle to be with, to accompany new friends in another culture, they discover both that culture, those friends, and their own culture and people in newer and deeper ways. For missioners from the United States, this experience is usually one of revelation, shock, and solidarity with the underside of life on this earth. The life and struggles that are discovered are not those of the misnamed Third World of so-called underdeveloped countries, but of the three-quarters of the world's peoples who are economically and politically not in control of their own lives, and militarily oppressed in the interest of "national security." It is a special privilege to be a missioner and to be invited to accompany missioners as they in turn seek to accompany their brothers and sisters through and beyond the barriers of poverty, language, culture, food, climate, oppression, and violence. This role of missioner is analogous to the service of pastoral counseling, which is also a relationship of life and faith through which a person or persons risk the uncovering of the unconnected and unintegrated segments of life in order to discover the Good News of life in abundance, and to recover through greater commitment and hope the possibility and energy to live and share this life. Barriers are broken down, and connections are made.

These words have been an attempt to name, describe, give some taste of one team and community expression of a life-giving process that has been and is taking place all over the world in every culture, country, and religion. God's Loving Spirit continues to call people together with one another and with creation through ever expanding *inclusion.* Differences are acknowledged, encouraged, and celebrated. Men and women and all creation come together not in competition but in mutual *empowerment.* Each relates to the other as a source of creative energy to be increased and communicated, rather than diminished and controlled. And finally, there is the movement toward communion of *partnership,* in which solidarity and creativity replace domination and violence.

Inclusion, empowerment, and partnership are some of the fruits of a creative pastoral counseling process; they seem to be indicators of the movement of God's Creating Spirit among people becoming community. Missioners seek to encourage and become part of this creative movement among the peoples they serve, within the cultures in which they live and to which they seek to adapt. In this movement the stranger becomes a friend — a brother or sister on the same journey. This is the movement of creative pastoral counseling within a culture, across cultures. There is always death as part of life; there is also hope in the face of death — courage to continue creating life anew in hope.

This appendix began with holy places; it ends with holy people. Two of the recent martyrs of El Salvador give their names to the hundreds of thousands of other "little people" all over the world who give hope to all of us. Elba Ramos was the woman who earned her living by cooking meals for the Jesuit faculty of the University of Central America in El Salvador; Celina Ramos, her 16-year-old daughter, assisted her. As a way of avoiding violence, they did not return home after preparing supper on the night of November 15, 1989. There was too much danger with shooting and fighting between the military and guerillas around the university campus. This was the only night they stayed in a guestroom near the Jesuit quarters — for safety. Early the next morning these two women suffered the same death as the six priests, simply because the military murderers sought to leave no witnesses. Yet Elba and Celina now live with their Jesuit brothers and all the other martyrs for the sake of justice. They are present in the memories and hearts of those inspired to continue the struggle for community of all people. As they now empower the living by their deaths, so are we all empowered to share life and to give life. As they found partnership with the known and famous victims of injustice in the violence of their deaths, so can all of us find energy to be partners.

Pastoral counseling is a creative relationship between people, bringing forth new life. It has taken many forms in its short history and will continue to evolve. Partnership pastoral counseling through invitation, situation, orientation, and reflection is but one expression of this relationship. There are other expressions not yet in writing, and many more to come.

BIBLIOGRAPHY

Anderson, R. S., ed. 1979. *Theological Foundations for Ministry.* Grand Rapids, Michigan: Eerdmans Publishing Co.

Appiah-Kubi K., and S. Torres, eds. 1979. *African Theology en Route.* Maryknoll, New York: Orbis Books.

Augsburger, David W. 1986. *Pastoral Counseling Across Cultures.* Philadelphia: Westminster Press.

Bandler, Richard, and John Grinder. 1975. *The Structure of Magic.* Palo Alto, California: Science and Behavior Books.

Bandler, Richard, and John Grinder. 1979. *Frogs into Princes.* Moab, Utah: Real People Press.

Barth, K. 1963. *Evangelical Theology: An Introduction.* New York: Holt Rinehart & Winston.

Bel A., Th. Jonkergouw. 1991. *Wegwijzer Psychologie in Nederland*, Assen: van Gorcum.

Belzen van, J. 1989. "What's in a Name? Pastor in psychologicis of Pastor cum Psychologia? Bij gelegenheid van de 70e verjaardag van W.J. Berger," *Praktische Theologie*, 16, 4, 491–493.

Bengu, S. 1984. "Colonized Mind." Unpublished paper presented during the African Week in Salzburg, Austria.

Boia, M. 1973. "The Case Worker's Need for Orientation to the Culture of the Client," *The Family* (October 1973).

Bradshaw, John. 1988. *Healing the Shame That Binds You.* Pompano Beach, Florida: Health Communications, Inc.

Browning, D. S. 1985. "Introduction to Pastoral Counseling." In Wicks, R., R. Parsons, and D. Capps. *Clinical Handbook of Pastoral Counseling*, New York: Paulist Press.

Busia, K. A., and D. Forde, eds. 1970. "The Ashanti," *African Worlds.* London: Oxford University Press.

Clinebell, H. 1966. *Basic Types of Pastoral Counseling.* Nashville, Tennessee: Abingdon Press.

Comas-Diaz, Lillian, and Ezra E. H. Griffith. 1988. *Clinical Guidelines in Cross-Cultural Mental Health.* New York: Wiley

Corey, G. 1982. *Theory and Practice of Counseling and Psychotherapy.* Monterey, California: Brooks/Cole Pub.

Day, M. W., ed. 1985. *The Socio-cultural Dimension of Mental Health*, New York: Vantage Press.

Debats, D., ed. 1988. *Psychotherapie en Zingeving Een Spectrum van Visies*, Amersfoort/Leuven: Acco.

Dickson, Kwesi A. 1984. *Theology in Africa.* Maryknoll, New York: Orbis Books.

Dijkhuis, J. H., J. H. M. Mooren. 1988. *Psychotherapie en Levensbeschouwing*, Baarn: Ambo.

Dijkstra, C., H. Van Donselaar. 1988. "Psychotherapie in Nederland 1. Geschiedenis van de psychotherapie van 1900 tot nu," *Psycholoog* 23, 1, 1–7.

Dinkmeyer, D. C., D. C. Dinkmeyer, Jr., and L. Sperry. 1987. *Adlerian Counseling and Psychotherapy*. Columbus, Ohio: Merril Publishing Co.

Dreikurs, R. R. 1950. *Fundamentals of Adlerian Psychology*. Chicago, Illinois: Alfred Adler Institute.

Ela, J. M. 1988. *My Faith as an African*. Maryknoll, New York: Orbis Books.

Ellis, Albert, and Robert A. Harper. 1975. *A New Guide to Rational Living*. Englewood Cliffs, New Jersey: Prentice-Hall.

Estadt, Barry K. 1983. *Pastoral Counseling*. Englewood Cliffs, New Jersey: Prentice-Hall.

Fanon, Frantz. 1968. *Wretched of the Earth*. New York: Grove Press.

Felling, A., J. Peters, O. Schreuder. 1982. "Identitatswandel in den Niederlanden," Kolner *Zeitschrift fur Soziologie and Sozialpsychologie* 34, 1, 26–53.

Ferguson, E. D. 1984. *Adlerian Theory, an Introduction*. Vancouver, British Columbia: Adlerian Psychology Association of British Columbia.

Firet, G. M. 1986. *Dynamics in Pastoring*. Grand Rapids, Michigan: Eerdmans Publishing Co.

Firet, J., W. J. Berger, H. J. M. Vossen. 1991. "Levende Documenten. Gesprekken met oud-trainees van de KPV," *Praktische Theologie* 18, 2, 78–93.

Frankl, Viktor. 1959. *From Death Camp to Existentialism*. Boston: Beacon Press.

Gibran, Kahlil. 1946 (originally published 1923). *The Prophet*. New York: Alfred A. Knopf.

Hall, Edward T. 1977. *Beyond Culture*. New York: Doubleday Anchor.

Harrigan, T. P. 1988. "Culture Shock with a Happy Ending," *Journal of Counselling and Development*.

Healy, J. 1981. *The Fifth Gospel*. Maryknoll, New York: Orbis Books.

Heitink, G. 1991. "Identitteit en competentie van de pastor. In het licht van de Klinische Pastorale Training." *Praktische Theologie* 18, 2, 12–28.

Hood, R. E. 1990. *Must God Remain Greek: African Cultures and God-talk*. Minneapolis: Fortress Press.

Imasogie, O. 1983. *Guidelines for Christian Theology in Africa*. Achimota, Ghana: African Christian Press.

Kegan, Robert. 1982. *The Evolving Self*. Cambridge, Massachusetts: Harvard.

Lartey, E. Y. 1987. *Pastoral Counseling in Inter-cultural Perspective*. Frankfurt am Main: Yerlag Peter Lang.

Lewis, L. J. 1984. "The Formative Experience of Waiting: Moving from Living in Illusion to Living with Reality." Doctoral dissertation, Institute of Formative Spirituality, Duquesne University, Pittsburgh.

Masamba Ma Mpolo, and W. Kalu. 1985. *The Rites of Growth*. Ibadan: DayStar Press.

May, Rollo. 1969. *Love and Will*. New York: Norton.

Mbiti, John. 1969a. *African Religions and Philosophy*. Nairobi, Kenya; London: Heinemann Co.

Mbiti, John. 1969b. *African Traditional Religions*. New York: Frederick A. Praeger Publishing Co.

Mpolo, M., and W. Kalu. 1985. *The Risk of Growth: Counseling and Pastoral Theology in the African Context.* Nairobi, Kenya: Uzima Press Limited.

Nida, Eugene A. 1982. *Customs and Cultures: Anthropology for Christian Missions.* Pasadena, California: William Carey Library.

Nouwen, Henri J. M. 1969. *Intimacy.* Notre Dame, Indiana: Fides Publishers.

Nouwen, Henri J. M. 1971. *Creative Ministry.* New York: Doubleday.

Nouwen, Henri J. M. 1972. *The Wounded Healer.* New York: Doubleday.

Okolo, C. B. 1978. *The African Church and Signs of the Times.* Eldoret, Kenya: Gaba Publications.

Olson, T. 1988. "Bifocality—and the Space Between," *Journal of Counseling and Development.*

Perls, Frederick S. 1972. *In and Out of the Garbage Pail.* Toronto, New York: Bantam Books.

Pobee, J. S. 1979. *Towards an African Theology.* Nashville, Tennessee: Abingdon Press.

Rattray, R. S. 1959. *Religion and Art in Ashanti.* London: Oxford University Press.

Ray, Benjamin C. 1976. *African Religions, Symbol, Ritual, and Community.* Englewood Cliffs, New Jersey: Prentice-Hall.

Rogers, Carl. 1961. *On Becoming a Person.* Boston: Houghton Mifflin.

Rogers, Carl. 1980. *A Way of Being.* Boston: Houghton Mifflin.

Roll, Samuel. 1991. Conference given at the Annual Convention of the Ameri-Association of Pastoral Counselors, Albuquerque, New Mexico (April).

Stewart, Edward C. 1972 (1979). *American Cultural Patterns: A Cross-Cultural Perspective.* LaGrange Park, Illinois: Intercultural Network.

Sue, Derald Wing. 1981. *Counseling the Culturally Different.* New York: Wiley.

Sue, Derald Wing, and David Sue. 1990. *Counseling the Culturally Different.* New York: Wiley.

Thurlings, J. M. 1978. *De wankele zuil. Nederlandse katholieken tussen assimilatie en pluralisme.* Tweede, vermeerderde druk. Deventer: Van Loghum Slaterus.

Thurlings, J. M. 1979. "Pluralism and Assimilation in the Netherlands, with special reference to Dutch Catholicism," *International Journal of Comparative Sociology* 20, 1–2, 82–100.

Ven van der, J. A. 1991. "De identiteit van pastorale counseling," *Praktische Theologie* 18, 2, 94–120.

Weiner, I. B. 1975. *Principles of Psychotherapy.* New York: Wiley.

Whitehead, James D., and Evelyn E. Whitehead. 1991. *The Promise of Partnership.* San Francisco: Harper San Francisco.

Wicks, Robert J. 1988. *Living Simply in an Anxious World.* New York: Paulist Press.

Williamson, Sydney G. 1974. *Akan Religion and the Christian Faith.* Accra: Ghana University Press.

ABOUT THE EDITORS

Dr. Robert Wicks is professor and director of program development for pastoral counseling at Loyola College in Maryland and recently also served on the visiting faculty of both Princeton Theological Seminary and Washington Theological Union. Dr. Wicks, who is a graduate of Hahnemann Medical College as well as Fairfield and St. John's Universities, has also taught in universities and in professional schools of psychology, medicine, social work, and nursing. In addition, he has directed mental health treatment programs in the United States and the Orient.

Dr. Wicks has published a number of books. He is the senior co-editor of the *Clinical Handbook of Pastoral Counseling,* and is author of the widely read book *Availability: The Problem and the Gift* and *Living Simply in an Anxious World.*

Dr. Wicks also maintains a private practice in Maryland, is book review editor for the National Association of Catholic Chaplains, is general editor of Paulist Press's *Integration Books: Studies in Pastoral Psychology, Theology, and Spirituality,* and is a member of both the editorial board of *Human Development* and the editorial committee of the *Journal of Pastoral Care.* His major areas of expertise include the integration of psychology and spirituality and pastoral counseling.

Dr. Barry K. Estadt, founder of pastoral counseling programs at Loyola College in Maryland, currently serves as professor and director of doctoral clinical education. Dr. Estadt is a Diplomate in Counseling Psychology with the American Board of Examiners in Professional Psychology, a Diplomate in Pastoral Counseling with the American Association of Pastoral Counselors, a member of the National Register of Health Service Providers in Psychology, and is licensed for the practice of psychology in Maryland and several others states.

Dr. Estadt has made numerous professional presentations, has contributed articles and chapters to a variety of publications, and has been recognized regionally and nationally for his contributions to the field of pastoral counseling. Awards include the Prestigious Award of the National Association of Catholic Chaplains for his pioneering work in training for ministry, the William C. Bier Award of Division 36 of the American Psychological Association for his work in the integration of religion and psychology, and the Howard County Chamber of Commerce Outstanding Educator's Award, for his personal impact on the lives and careers of residents of the area.

Dr. Estadt's primary contributions in terms of publication are *Pastoral Counseling* with Prentice Hall and *The Art of Clinical Supervision: A Pastoral Counseling Perspective* with Paulist Press.

In addition to teaching, writing, lecturing, and supervising, Dr. Estadt serves as clinical director of Centennial Counseling, a multi-faceted, holistic counseling service that seeks to help people lead happier, healthier, more productive lives.